OL

HOROSCOPE AND ASTRAL DIARY

SCORPIO

foulsham
LONDON • NEW YORK • TORONTO • SYDNEY

foulsham
Capital Point, 33 Bath Road, Slough, Berkshire, SL1 3UF, England

Foulsham books can be found in all good bookshops and direct from
www.foulsham.com

ISBN: 978-0-572-04009-3

A CIP record for this book is available from the British Library

Printed in Great Britain by CPI Group (UK) Ltd, Croydon, CR0 4YY.

CONTENTS

INTRODUCTION

In the midst of our busy lives we often fail to notice the subtle changes within our natures that take place on an almost moment-by-moment basis. Some of these are the natural result of circumstances, but others are a direct response to the constantly changing patterns of the Sun, Moon and planets. Astrology gives us an opportunity to make the very best of what cosmological forces are acting upon us at any particular point in time, and Old Moore has been tracking planetary movements and the bearing they have on humanity for many centuries. The most recent result of his efforts is the Astral Diary for 2013 – a complete book geared specifically towards you and the influences that help to make you what you are.

If you want to know whether a new relationship is likely to turn out the way you hope, whether you are in for a good time in the financial stakes, or whether family pressures could be a problem, Old Moore is the person to ask. The Astral Diary gives you an easy-to-follow daily summary of the way the stars and planets are affecting you, and also tells you what you should be doing now in order to maximise your potential for the future. And there is also space in the diaries for your own comments and appointments.

The Astral Diary allows you to look much deeper into your own individual nature than other yearly forecasts do. Your uniqueness is reflected by the time of day you were born and by the position of specific heavenly bodies such as the Moon and the planet Venus. Using the Astral Diary's unique tables you can work out what makes you tick in a much more personal sense, and can then deal much more effectively with the twists and turns of life.

Every nuance of your nature is captured within your astrological profile, and using the Astral Diary you can get so close to the core of planetary influence that you can almost feel the subtle undertones that, in the end, have a profound bearing on your life and circumstances. It is even possible to register when little Mercury is 'retrograde', which means that it appears to be moving backwards in space when viewed from the Earth. Mercury rules communication, so be prepared to deal with a few setbacks in this area when you see the sign ☿. Used correctly, astrology allows you to maximise your potential, to strike whilst the iron is hot and to live a more contented and successful life. Consulting *Old Moore's Astral Diary* will make you more aware of what really makes you the person you are and is a fascinating way to register the very heartbeat of the solar system of which we are all a part.

Old Moore extends his customary greeting to all people of the Earth and offers his age-old wishes for a happy and prosperous period ahead.

THE ESSENCE OF SCORPIO

Exploring the Personality of Scorpio the Scorpion

(24th OCTOBER – 22nd NOVEMBER)

What's in a sign?

To say that you are a little complicated and somewhat difficult to understand is probably a great understatement. The basic reason for this lies in the peculiar nature of Scorpio rulership. In terms of the elements, your zodiac sign is a Water sign. This makes you naturally emotional, deep, somewhat reserved and ever anxious to help those around you. As a direct contrast, classical astrologers always maintained that your planetary ruler was Mars. Mars is the planet of combat and aggression, being positive and dominant under most circumstances. So it can be judged from the start that there are great contradictions within the basic Scorpio nature.

It's a fact that many people are naturally cautious of Scorpio people. Perhaps this isn't surprising. Under most circumstances you appear to be quiet and peaceful, but the situation is a little like a smoking bomb. When it comes to defending yourself, or in particular those people who you see as being important to you, there is virtually no limit to which you would refuse to go. Generally speaking our ancient ancestors were extremely wise in terms of the names they gave to the different zodiac signs. Consider the apparently diminutive and retiring scorpion. It doesn't go looking for trouble and is generally happy to remain in the shadows. However, if it is provoked, or even attacked, it will take on adversaries many times its own size. It carries a barbed sting in its tail and will strike without any additional warning if necessary.

All the same, the Scorpio reputation may be a little undeserved. Yours is one of the most compassionate and caring of all the zodiac signs. When it comes to working on behalf of humanity, especially the oppressed, the sick or the disenfranchised, you show your true mettle. You cannot stand the thought of people suffering unjustifiably, which is why many of the great social reformers and even freedom fighters had the same zodiac sign as you do.

As a Scorpio you are likely to be intuitive (some would say psychic) and under most circumstances you are more than willing to follow that little voice inside yourself that tells you how to behave in any given situation.

Scorpio resources

Your nature is so very often understated that it might be said that your greatest resource is surprise. You have the ability to shock people constantly, even those who think they understand you perfectly well. This brings us back to the creature for which your zodiac sign is named. A scorpion is diminutive – and would represent a tasty snack for any would-be predator. However, it defies logic by standing its ground and fighting back. When it does, woe betide the aggressor that refuses to take account of its presence. And so it is with you. Quiet, even reserved, you tend to get on with your work. This you do efficiently and without undue fuss, approaching each task with the same methodical attitude. People often don't even realise that you are around. And then, when they least expect it, there you are!

The ability to surprise means that you often get on in life against heavy odds. In addition you have great resilience and fortitude. It is possible for you to continue to work long and hard under circumstances that would force others to retreat. Most Scorpio people would not consider themselves to be tough – in fact quite a few are positively neurotic when it comes to matters associated with their own health. Yet you can endure hardship well and almost always win through in the end.

It's true that you may not be quite as confident as you could be. If you were, people would notice you more and that would detract from that all-important element of surprise that makes you so formidable, and which is definitely the most important weapon in your armoury. However, it is clear that your greatest resource is compassion, and on those occasions when you really allow it to show, you display yourself as being one of the most important allies to your fellow men and women.

At a practical level you are more than capable and can often be expected to perform tasks that you haven't necessarily undertaken before. You have a deep intelligence and good powers to reason things out. Most important of all is a determination that no other zodiac sign can match.

Beneath the surface

This section of an account of the typical Scorpio nature could fill an entire book in itself because you are such a complicated person. However, there are certain advantages to being a Scorpio. For example, nobody is going to run away with the idea that you are basically uncomplicated and shallow. It ought to be clear enough to the dullest observer that there is a boiling, seething volcano bubbling away beneath the surface of almost every Scorpio subject.

You are often accused of having a slightly dark view of life, and it's true that many Scorpio people enjoy a rather morbid curiosity and are fascinated by subjects that make other people shudder. At the same time you could hardly be described as being one of life's natural optimists. Part of the reason for this lies in the fact that you have been disappointed in the past and may have arrived at the conclusion that to expect the worst is often the most sensible course of action. At least that way you are likely to mitigate some of the potential depression regarding failures in the future.

Although this way of thinking is somewhat faulty, it comes so naturally to the Scorpio subject that it actually works very well, though it has to be said that it might be responsible for a tendency to hold back on occasions. Assessing the way your inner mind works is as difficult for you as it is for any outsider. Even individuals who have been friends for years will sometimes come desperately unstuck if they arrive at the conclusion that they know well what makes you tick. In the recesses of your mind you are passionate, driving, restless, dissatisfied and frequently disappointed with your own efforts. On the other hand, you have the power to make dreams into realities and are excellent at hatching plans that will benefit people far from your own circle and circumstances. Being a tireless worker on behalf of the oppressed, the fate of humanity as a whole is ever an inner concern.

When you love you do so with great width and depth. Your capacity for jealousy knows no bounds and there are times when you can be as destructive to yourself as you ever could be regarding any other individual. Yet for all this your inner mind is lofty and can soar like an eagle on occasions. If the world at large was able to fathom just one tenth of the way your inner mind actually works, people would find you even more fascinating than they do already. But perhaps it's best that they don't. The deepest recesses of Scorpio are an intense secret and will usually stay that way.

Making the best of yourself

It isn't hard to find a single word that describes the way you can make the best of yourself, especially when viewed by the world at large. That word is 'communication'. When difficulties arise in your life, especially concerning other people, it's usually because you haven't managed to get your message across, and probably because you haven't even tried to do so. There is much to your nature that is electric, powerful and magnetic. These qualities make you potentially popular and fascinating to a wealth of individuals. Hide these qualities beneath too brusque an exterior and you can seem dark and brooding.

Of course it's a fine line and one that isn't easy to walk. You are constantly worried that if you show people what really makes you tick, they will not find you interesting at all. In reality this concern is totally without foundation. There is more than enough depth about you to last several lifetimes. It doesn't matter how much you give of yourself to the world at large, there are always going to be surprises galore to follow.

Use the dynamic qualities of your nature to the full. Traditionally your ruling planet is Mars – a real go-getter of a planetary ruler and one that imbues you with tremendous power to get things done at a practical level. On the way you need to show how much you care about others. Amidst a plethora of gifts offered to you by the celestial spheres, your ability to help others is likely to be top of the list. When you are giving you are also usually approachable. For you the two go hand in hand. Avoid allowing yourself to become morose or inward looking and always strive to find simple answers to simple questions.

Stick to some sort of work that you find interesting. That can be almost anything to a Scorpio, as long as it feeds the inner you. It does need to carry a degree of diversity and should ideally have an end product that is easy to see. On your journey through life don't get carried away with daydreams – yet on the other hand avoid losing your great potential to make them come true.

The impressions you give

This is one area of your life over which you do have a great deal of control. If the adage 'what you see is what you get' turns out to be true for many signs of the zodiac, it certainly isn't the case with you. The complexity of your nature makes it difficult for even you to find 'the real Scorpio', and in any case this tends to change from day to day. However, regarding some matters there isn't any doubt at all. Firstly you are deeply magnetic and possess the ability to arouse an instinctive fascination in others. Ally this to your propensity for being very positive in your decision making and you have a potentially formidable combination.

Most people already think of you as being an extremely interesting person. Unfortunately they may also occasionally consider you to be a little cool and somewhat difficult to approach. Neither of these impressions are true, it's simply that you are quite shy at heart, and sometimes find it difficult to believe that you could be liked by certain individuals. Learn to throw this erroneous assumption out of the window, and instead, expect to be viewed positively. To do so would make all the difference and would clear the way so that your more personable side can show all the time.

Very few people who know you well could fail to realise that you care deeply, especially about the well-being of the oppressed. You have a truly noble spirit, a fact that shines through in practically everything you do – yet another reason to be noticed.

It's true that you can sometimes make your secretive quality into an art form, which those looking in from the outside might find rather difficult to deal with. This represents another outward aspect of your nature that could so easily be altered. By all means keep your secrets, though not about matters that are of no real note whatsoever. In a single phrase, try to lighten up a little. It's all you need to be almost perfect!

The way forward

It must first be held in mind that Scorpio people are complicated. That's something you simply cannot get away from, no matter how much you might try. On the one hand you can deal with practical matters almost instinctively. You are resourceful, deep thinking, intense and fascinating. On the other side of the coin you are often too fond of luxury and will frequently withdraw yourself from situations that you do not care to pursue. You can be quite stubborn and can even bear a grudge if you feel that you have been provoked.

It is suggested in astrology that no quality of nature is necessarily good or bad, it really depends on the way it is used. For example, stubbornness can be considered a terrible fault, but not if you were being awkward concerning the obvious rights of an oppressed person or group. It turns out that Scorpio has more of a potential to be 'saint or sinner' than any zodiac sign. As long as you examine your motives in any given situation, whilst at the same time trying to cultivate a degree of flexibility that is not one of your natural gifts, then you won't go far wrong.

Turn on the charm when it is necessary because it will rarely if ever let you down. Think about the way you can serve the world, but don't preach about it. Love sincerely, but don't allow jealousy to spoil things. Be constructive in your determination and don't get on your high horse when it isn't necessary. Follow these simple rules for the best chance of progress.

Of course there are many positives around to start with. You are a very loyal friend, are capable of being extremely brave and tend to be very committed to family members. At the same time you are trustworthy and can work long and hard using your own initiative. Although you sometimes worry about your health, you are more robust than most and can endure a high degree of hardship if necessary. You don't take kindly to criticism but can be flexible enough to accept it if you know it is intended for your own good.

Few people doubt your sincerity – that is, when they know what you believe. So it's important to lay your thoughts on the line right from the start. And even if you don't choose to treat the whole world as a friend, you are capable of gathering a little circle around you who would never let you down. Do make sure, however, that this 'inner group' isn't simply comprised of other Scorpios!

SCORPIO ON THE CUSP

Old Moore is often asked how astrological profiles are altered for those people born at either the beginning or the end of a zodiac sign, or, more properly, on the cusps of a sign. In the case of Scorpio this would be on the 24th of October and for two or three days after, and similarly at the end of the sign, probably from the 20th to the 22nd of November. In this year's Astral Diaries, once again, Old Moore sets out to explain the differences regarding cuspid signs.

The Libra Cusp – October 24th to 26th

You are probably generally considered to be a bright and breezy sort of character, with a great deal of enthusiasm for life. Despite this, few people would doubt that you are a shrewd operator, and that you know what you want and have a fairly good idea of how to go about getting it. Not everyone likes you as much as you would wish, but that's because the Libran side of your nature longs for popularity, while set against this is your deep Scorpio need to speak your mind, even when you know that other people might wish you did not indulge in this trait very frequently. In love, you typify the split between these two signs. On the one hand you are passionate, sincere and intense, while on the other your Libran responses can cause a certain fickle sort of affection to show sometimes, probably to the confusion of those with whom you are involved at a personal level. Nevertheless, few people would find fault with your basic nature and there isn't much doubt that your heart is in the right place.

When it comes to career matters, you have a very fortunate combination. Scorpio can sometimes be accused of lacking diplomacy, but nothing could be further from the truth with Libra. As a result, you have what it takes in terms of determination but at the same time you are capable of seeing the point of view put forward by colleagues. You tend to rise to the top of the tree and, with your mixture of raw ability and humour that most of the world approves of, you can stay there.

You won't be the sort of person to make quite as many enemies as Scorpio taken alone might do, and you need the cut and thrust of the world much more than the retiring creature after whom your zodiac sign is named. Try not to be controversial and do your best to retain a sense of humour, which is essential to your well-being. Few would doubt the fact that your heart is in the right place and your creative potential could be second to none. Most important of all, you need the self-satisfaction that comes from living in the real world.

The Sagittarius Cusp – November 20th to 22nd

You can be a really zany character, with a love of life that is second to none. Add to this a penetrating insight, a razor-sharp wit and an instinctive intuition that is quite remarkable and we find in you a formidable person. It's true that not everyone understands what makes you tick, probably least of all yourself, but you strive to be liked and really do want to advertise your willingness to learn and to grow, which isn't always the province of Scorpio when taken alone. Your capacity for work knows no bounds, though you don't really like to get your hands dirty and would feel more content when telling others what to do.

In a career sense, you need to be in a position from which you are able to delegate. This is not because you are afraid of hard work yourself, far from it, but you possess a strong ability to see through problems and you are a natural director of others. Sales careers may interest you, or a position from which you can organise and arrange things. However, you hate to be tied down to one place for long, so you would be at your best when allowed to move around freely and do things in your own way.

You are a natural social reformer, mainly because you are sure that you know what is right and just. In the main you are correct in your assumptions, but there are occasions when you should realise that there is more than one form of truth. Perhaps you are not always quite as patient with certain individuals as you might be but these generally tend to be people who show traits of cruelty or cunning. As a family person, you care very much for the people who figure most prominently in your life. Sometimes you are a definite home bird, with a preference for what you know and love, but this is offset by a restless trend within your nature that often sends you off into the wide blue yonder, chasing rainbows that the Scorpio side of your nature doubts are even there. Few would doubt your charm, your magnetism, or your desire to get ahead in life in almost any way possible. You combine patience with genuine talent and make a loyal, interesting and entertaining friend or lover.

SCORPIO AND ITS ASCENDANTS

The nature of every individual on the planet is composed of the rich variety of zodiac signs and planetary positions that were present at the time of their birth. Your Sun sign, which in your case is Scorpio, is one of the many factors when it comes to assessing the unique person you are. Probably the most important consideration, other than your Sun sign, is to establish the zodiac sign that was rising over the eastern horizon at the time that you were born. This is your Ascending or Rising sign. Most popular astrology fails to take account of the Ascendant, and yet its importance remains with you from the very moment of your birth, through every day of your life. The Ascendant is evident in the way you approach the world, and so, when meeting a person for the first time, it is this astrological influence that you are most likely to notice first. Our Ascending sign essentially represents what we appear to be, while the Sun sign is what we feel inside ourselves.

The Ascendant also has the potential for modifying our overall nature. For example, if you were born at a time of day when Scorpio was passing over the eastern horizon (this would be around the time of dawn) then you would be classed as a double Scorpio. As such, you would typify this zodiac sign, both internally and in your dealings with others. However, if your Ascendant sign turned out to be a Fire sign, such as Aries, there would be a profound alteration of nature, away from the expected qualities of Scorpio.

One of the reasons why popular astrology often ignores the Ascendant is that it has always been rather difficult to establish. Old Moore has found a way to make this possible by devising an easy-to-use table, which you will find on page 158 of this book. Using this, you can establish your Ascendant sign at a glance. You will need to know your rough time of birth, then it is simply a case of following the instructions.

For those readers who have no idea of their time of birth it might be worth allowing a good friend, or perhaps your partner, to read through the section that follows this introduction. Someone who deals with you on a regular basis may easily discover your Ascending sign, even though you could have some difficulty establishing it for yourself. A good understanding of this component of your nature is essential if you want to be aware of that 'other person' who is responsible for the way you make contact with the world at large. Your Sun sign, Ascendant sign, and the other pointers in this book will, together, allow you a far better understanding of what makes you tick as an individual. Peeling back the different layers of your astrological make-up can be an enlightening experience, and the Ascendant may represent one of the most important layers of all.

Scorpio with Scorpio Ascendant

This is one of the most potent of all astrological possibilities, but how it is used depends so very much on the individual who possesses it. On the one hand you are magnetic, alluring, sexy, deep and very attractive, whilst at the same time you are capable of being stubborn, self-seeking, vain, over-sensitive and fathomless. It has to be said that under most circumstances the first set of adjectives are the most appropriate, and that is because you keep control of the deeper side, refusing to allow it absolute control over your conscious life. You are able to get almost anything you want from life, but first you have to discover what that might be. The most important factor of all, however, is the way you can offer yourself, totally and without reservation to a needy world.

Self-sacrifice is a marvellous thing, but you can go too far on occasions. The furthest extreme for Scorpios here is a life that is totally dedicated to work and prayer. For the few this is admirable, for the still earth-based, less so. Finding a compromise is not easy as you are not always in touch with yourself. Feed the spiritual, curb the excesses, accept the need for luxury, and be happy.

Scorpio with Sagittarius Ascendant

There are many gains with this combination, and most of you reading this will already be familiar with the majority of them. Sagittarius offers a bright and hopeful approach to life, but may not always have the staying power and the patience to get what it really needs. Scorpio, on the other hand, can be too deep for its own good, is very self-seeking on occasions and extremely giving to others. Both the signs have problems when taken on their own, and, it has to be said, double the difficulties when they come together. But this is not usually the case. Invariably the presence of Scorpio slows down the over-quick responses of the Archer, whilst the inclusion of Sagittarius prevents Scorpio from taking itself too seriously.

Life is so often a game of extremes, when all the great spiritual masters of humanity have indicated that a 'middle way' is the path to choose. You have just the right combination of skills and mental faculties to find that elusive path, and can bring great joy to yourself and others as a result. Most of the time you are happy, optimistic, helpful and a joy to know. You have mental agility, backed up by a stunning intuition, which itself would rarely let you down. Keep a sense of proportion and understand that your depth of intellect is necessary to curb your flighty side.

Scorpio with Capricorn Ascendant

If patience, perseverance and a solid ability to get where you want to go are considered to be the chief components of a happy life, then you should be skipping about every day. Unfortunately this is not always the case and here we have two zodiac signs, both of which can be too deep for their own good. Both Scorpio and Capricorn are inclined to take themselves rather too seriously and your main lesson in life, and some would say the reason you have adopted this zodiac combination, is to 'lighten up'. If all that determination is pushed in the direction of your service to the world at large, you are seen as being one of the kindest people imaginable. This is really the only option for you, because if you turn this tremendous potential power inwards all the time you will become brooding, secretive and sometimes even selfish. Your eyes should be turned towards a needy humanity, which can be served with the dry but definite wit of Capricorn and the true compassion of Scorpio.

It is impossible with this combination to indicate what areas of life suit you the best. Certainly you adore luxury in all its forms, and yet you can get by with almost nothing. You desire travel, and at the same time love the comforts and stability of home. The people who know you best are aware that you are rather special. Listen to what they say.

Scorpio with Aquarius Ascendant

Here we have a combination that shows much promise and a flexibility that allows many changes in direction, allied to a power to succeed, sometimes very much against all the odds. Aquarius lightens the load of the Scorpio mind, turning the depths into potential and making intuitive foresight into a means for getting on in life. There are depths here, because even airy Aquarius isn't too easy to understand, and it is therefore a fact that some people with this combination will always be something of a mystery. However, even this fact can be turned to your advantage because it means that people will always be looking at you. Confidence is so often the key to success in life and the Scorpio–Aquarius mix offers this, or at least appears to do so. Even when this is not entirely the case, the fact that everyone around you believes it to be true is often enough.

You are usually good to know, and show a keen intellect and a deep intelligence, aided by a fascination for life that knows no bounds. When at your best you are giving, understanding, balanced and active. On those occasions when things are not going well for you, beware a stubborn streak and the need to be sensational. Keep it light and happy and you won't go far wrong. Most of you are very, very well loved.

Scorpio with Pisces Ascendant

You stand a chance of disappearing so deep into yourself that other people would need one of those long ladders that cave explorers use, just to find you. It isn't really your fault because both Scorpio and Pisces are Water signs, which are difficult to understand, and you have them both. But that doesn't mean that you should be content to remain in the dark, and the warmth of your nature is all you need to shine a light on the wonderful qualities you possess. But the primary word of warning is that you must put yourself on display and allow others to know what you are, before their appreciation of these facts becomes apparent.

As a server of the world you are second to none and it is hard to find a person with this combination who is not, in some way, looking out for the people around them. Immensely attractive to others, you are also one of the most sought-after lovers. Much of this has to do with your deep and abiding charm, but the air of mystery that surrounds you also helps. Some of you will marry too early, and end up regretting the fact, though the majority of people with Scorpio and Pisces will find the love they deserve in the end. You are able, just, firm but fair, though a sucker for a hard luck story and as kind as the day is long. It's hard to imagine how so many good points could be ignored by others.

Scorpio with Aries Ascendant

The two very different faces of Mars come together in this potent, magnetic and quite awe-inspiring combination. Your natural inclination is towards secrecy, and this fact, together with the natural attractions of the sensual Scorpio nature, makes you the object of great curiosity. This means that you will not go short of attention and should ensure that you are always being analysed by people who may never get to know you at all. At heart you prefer your own company, and yet life appears to find means to push you into the public gaze time and again. Most people with this combination ooze sex appeal and can use this fact as a stepping stone to personal success, yet without losing any integrity or loosening the cords of a deeply moralistic nature.

On those occasions when you do lose your temper, there isn't a character in the length and breadth of the zodiac who would have either the words or the courage to stand against the stream of invective that follows. On really rare occasions you might even scare yourself. A simple look is enough to show family members when you are not amused. Few people are left unmoved by your presence in their life.

Scorpio with Taurus Ascendant

The first, last and most important piece of advice for you is not to take yourself, or anyone else, too seriously. This might be rather a tall order because Scorpio intensifies the deeper qualities of Taurus and can make you rather lacking in the sense of humour that we all need to live our lives in this most imperfect of worlds. You are naturally sensual by nature. This shows itself in a host of ways. In all probability you can spend hours in the bath, love to treat yourself to good food and drink and take your greatest pleasure in neat and orderly surroundings. This can often alienate you from those who live in the same house because other people need to use the bathroom from time to time and they cannot remain tidy indefinitely.

You tend to worry a great deal about things which are really not too important, but don't take this statement too seriously or you will begin to worry about this fact too! You often need to lighten up and should always do your best to tell yourself that most things are not half so important as they seem to be. Be careful over the selection of a life partner and if possible choose someone who is naturally funny and who does not take life anywhere near as seriously as you are inclined to do. At work you are more than capable and in all probability everyone relies heavily on your wise judgements.

Scorpio with Gemini Ascendant

What you are and what you appear to be can be two entirely different things with this combination. Although you appear to be every bit as chatty and even as flighty as Gemini tends to be, nothing could be further from the truth. In reality you have many deep and penetrating insights, all of which are geared towards sorting out potential problems before they come along. Few people would have the ability to pull the wool over your eyes, and you show a much more astute face to the world than is often the case for Gemini taken on its own. The level of your confidence, although not earth-shattering, is much greater with this combination, and you would not be thwarted once you had made up your mind.

There is a slight danger here, however, because Gemini is always inclined to nerve problems of one sort or another. In the main these are slight and fleeting, though the presence of Scorpio can intensify reactions and heighten the possibility of depression, which would not be at all fortunate. The best way round this potential problem is to have a wealth of friends, plenty to do and the sort of variety in your life that suits your Mercury ruler. Financial success is not too difficult to achieve because you can easily earn money and then manage to hold on to it.

Scorpio with Cancer Ascendant

There are few more endearing zodiac combinations than this one. Both signs are Watery in nature and show a desire to work on behalf of humanity as a whole. The world sees you as being genuinely caring, full of sympathy for anyone in trouble and always ready to lend a hand when it is needed. You are a loyal friend, a great supporter of the oppressed and a lover of home and family. In a work sense you are capable, and command respect from your colleagues, even though this comes about courtesy of your quiet competence and not as a result of anything that you might happen to say.

But we should not get too carried away with external factors, or the way that others see you. Inside you are a boiling pool of emotion. You feel more strongly, love more deeply and hurt more fully than any other combination of the Water signs. Even those who think they know you really well would get a shock if they could take a stroll around the deeper recesses of your mind. Although these facts are true, they may be rather beside the point because it is a fact that the truth of your passion, commitment and deep convictions may only surface fully half a dozen times in your life. The fact is that you are a very private person at heart and you don't know how to be any other way.

Scorpio with Leo Ascendant

A Leo with intensity, that's what you are. You are mad about good causes and would argue the hind leg off a donkey in defence of your many ideals. If you are not out there saving the planet you could just be at home in the bath, thinking up the next way to save humanity from its own worst excesses. In your own life, although you love little luxuries, you are sparing and frugal, yet generous as can be to those you take to. It's a fact that you don't like everyone, and of course the same is true in reverse. It might be easier for you to understand why you can dislike than to appreciate the reverse side of the coin, for your pride can be badly dented on occasions. Scorpio brings a tendency to have down spells, though the fact that Leo is also strongly represented in your nature should prevent them from becoming a regular part of your life.

It is important for you to learn how to forgive and forget, and there isn't much point in bearing a grudge because you are basically too noble to do so. If something goes wrong, kiss the situation goodbye and get on with the next interesting adventure, of which there are many in your life. Stop–start situations sometimes get in the way, but there are plenty of people around who would be only too willing to lend a helping hand.

Scorpio with Virgo Ascendant

This is intensity carried through to the absolute. If you have a problem, it is that you fail to externalise all that is going on inside that deep, bubbling cauldron that is your inner self. Realising what you are capable of is not a problem; these only start when you have to make it plain to those around you what you want. Part of the reason for this is that you don't always understand yourself. You love intensely and would do absolutely anything for a person you are fond of, even though you might have to inconvenience yourself a great deal on the way. Relationships can cause you slight problems however, since you need to associate with people who at least come somewhere near to understanding what makes you tick. If you manage to bridge the gap between yourself and the world that constantly knocks on your door, you show yourself to be powerful, magnetic and compulsive.

There are times when you definitely prefer to stay quiet, though you do have a powerful ability to get your message across when you think it is necessary to do so. There are people around who might think that you are a push-over but they could easily get a shock when you sense that the time is right to answer back. You probably have a very orderly house and don't care for clutter of any sort.

Scorpio with Libra Ascendant

There is some tendency for you to be far more deep than the average Libran would appear to be and for this reason it is crucial that you lighten up from time to time. Every person with a Scorpio quality needs to remember that there is a happy and carefree side to all events and your Libran quality should allow you to bear this in mind. Sometimes you try to do too many things at the same time. This is fine if you take the casual overview of Libra, but less sensible when you insist on picking the last bone out of every potential, as is much more the case for Scorpio.

When worries come along, as they sometimes will, be able to listen to what your friends have to say and also realise that they are more than willing to work on your behalf, if only because you are so loyal to them. You do have a quality of self-deception, but this should not get in the way too much if you combine the instinctive actions of Libra with the deep intuition of your Scorpio component.

Probably the most important factor of this combination is your ability to succeed in a financial sense. You make a good manager, but not of the authoritarian sort. Jobs in the media or where you are expected to make up your mind quickly would suit you, because there is always an underpinning of practical sense that rarely lets you down.

THE MOON AND THE PART IT PLAYS IN YOUR LIFE

In astrology the Moon is probably the single most important heavenly body after the Sun. Its unique position, as partner to the Earth on its journey around the solar system, means that the Moon appears to pass through the signs of the zodiac extremely quickly. The zodiac position of the Moon at the time of your birth plays a great part in personal character and is especially significant in the build-up of your emotional nature.

Sun Moon Cycles

The first lunar cycle deals with the part the position of the Moon plays relative to your Sun sign. I have made the fluctuations of this pattern easy for you to understand by means of a simple cyclic graph. It appears on the first page of each 'Your Month At A Glance', under the title 'Highs and Lows'. The graph displays the lunar cycle and you will soon learn to understand how its movements have a bearing on your level of energy and your abilities.

Your Own Moon Sign

Discovering the position of the Moon at the time of your birth has always been notoriously difficult because tracking the complex zodiac positions of the Moon is not easy. This process has been reduced to three simple stages with Old Moore's unique Lunar Tables. A breakdown of the Moon's zodiac positions can be found from page 25 onwards, so that once you know what your Moon Sign is, you can see what part this plays in the overall build-up of your personal character.

If you follow the instructions on the next page you will soon be able to work out exactly what zodiac sign the Moon occupied on the day that you were born and you can then go on to compare the reading for this position with those of your Sun sign and your Ascendant. It is partly the comparison between these three important positions that goes towards making you the unique individual you are.

HOW TO DISCOVER YOUR MOON SIGN

This is a three-stage process. You may need a pen and a piece of paper but if you follow the instructions below the process should only take a minute or so.

STAGE 1 First of all you need to know the Moon Age at the time of your birth. If you look at Moon Table 1, on page 23, you will find all the years between 1915 and 2013 down the left side. Find the year of your birth and then trace across to the right to the month of your birth. Where the two intersect you will find a number. This is the date of the New Moon in the month that you were born. You now need to count forward the number of days between the New Moon and your own birthday. For example, if the New Moon in the month of your birth was shown as being the 6th and you were born on the 20th, your Moon Age Day would be 14. If the New Moon in the month of your birth came after your birthday, you need to count forward from the New Moon in the previous month. Whatever the result, jot this number down so that you do not forget it.

STAGE 2 Take a look at Moon Table 2 on page 24. Down the left hand column look for the date of your birth. Now trace across to the month of your birth. Where the two meet you will find a letter. Copy this letter down alongside your Moon Age Day.

STAGE 3 Moon Table 3 on page 24 will supply you with the zodiac sign the Moon occupied on the day of your birth. Look for your Moon Age Day down the left hand column and then for the letter you found in Stage 2. Where the two converge you will find a zodiac sign and this is the sign occupied by the Moon on the day that you were born.

Your Zodiac Moon Sign Explained

You will find a profile of all zodiac Moon Signs on pages 25 to 28, showing in yet another way how astrology helps to make you into the individual that you are. In each daily entry of the Astral Diary you can find the zodiac position of the Moon for every day of the year. This also allows you to discover your lunar birthdays. Since the Moon passes through all the signs of the zodiac in about a month, you can expect something like twelve lunar birthdays each year. At these times you are likely to be emotionally steady and able to make the sort of decisions that have real, lasting value.

MOON TABLE 1

YEAR	SEP	OCT	NOV	YEAR	SEP	OCT	NOV	YEAR	SEP	OCT	NOV
1915	9	8	7	1948	3	2	1	1981	28	27	26
1916	27	27	26	1949	23	21	20	1982	17	17	15
1917	15	15	14	1950	12	11	9	1983	7	6	4
1918	4	4	3	1951	1	1/30	29	1984	25	24	22
1919	23	23	22	1952	19	18	17	1985	14	14	12
1920	12	12	10	1953	8	8	6	1986	4	3	2
1921	2	1/30	29	1954	27	26	25	1987	23	22	21
1922	21	20	19	1955	16	15	14	1988	11	10	9
1923	10	10	8	1956	4	4	2	1989	29	29	28
1924	28	28	26	1957	23	23	21	1990	19	18	17
1925	18	17	16	1958	13	12	11	1991	8	8	6
1926	7	6	5	1959	3	2/31	30	1992	26	25	24
1927	25	25	24	1960	21	20	19	1993	16	15	14
1928	14	14	12	1961	10	9	8	1994	5	5	3
1929	3	2	1	1962	28	28	27	1995	24	24	22
1930	22	20	19	1963	17	17	15	1996	13	11	10
1931	12	11	9	1964	6	5	4	1997	2	2/31	30
1932	30	29	27	1965	25	24	22	1998	20	20	19
1933	19	19	17	1966	14	14	12	1999	9	9	8
1934	9	8	7	1967	4	3	2	2000	27	27	26
1935	27	27	26	1968	23	22	21	2001	17	17	16
1936	15	15	14	1969	11	10	9	2002	6	6	4
1937	4	4	3	1970	1	1/30	29	2003	26	25	24
1938	23	23	22	1971	19	19	18	2004	13	12	11
1939	13	12	11	1972	8	8	6	2005	3	2	1
1940	2	1/30	29	1973	27	26	25	2006	22	21	20
1941	21	20	19	1974	16	15	14	2007	12	11	9
1942	10	10	8	1975	5	5	3	2008	30	29	28
1943	29	29	27	1976	23	23	21	2009	19	18	17
1944	17	17	15	1977	13	12	11	2010	8	8	6
1945	6	6	4	1978	2	2/31	30	2011	27	27	25
1946	25	24	23	1979	21	20	19	2012	6	15	13
1947	14	14	12	1980	10	9	8	2013	4	4	2

TABLE 2

DAY	OCT	NOV
1	a	e
2	a	e
3	a	e
4	b	f
5	b	f
6	b	f
7	b	f
8	b	f
9	b	f
10	b	f
11	b	f
12	b	f
13	b	g
14	d	g
15	d	g
16	d	g
17	d	g
18	d	g
19	d	g
20	d	g
21	d	g
22	d	g
23	d	i
24	e	i
25	e	i
26	e	i
27	e	i
28	e	i
29	e	i
30	e	i
31	e	–

TABLE 3

M/D	a	b	d	e	f	g	i
0	LI	LI	LI	SC	SC	SC	SA
1	LI	LI	SC	SC	SC	SA	SA
2	LI	SC	SC	SC	SA	SA	CP
3	SC	SC	SC	SA	SA	CP	CP
4	SC	SA	SA	SA	CP	CP	CP
5	SA	SA	SA	CP	CP	AQ	AQ
6	SA	CP	CP	CP	AQ	AQ	AQ
7	SA	CP	CP	AQ	AQ	PI	PI
8	CP	CP	CP	AQ	PI	PI	PI
9	CP	AQ	AQ	AQ	PI	PI	AR
10	AQ	AQ	AQ	PI	AR	AR	AR
11	AQ	PI	PI	PI	AR	AR	TA
12	PI	PI	PI	AR	TA	TA	TA
13	PI	AR	PI	AR	TA	TA	GE
14	AR	AR	AR	TA	GE	GE	GE
15	AR	AR	AR	TA	TA	TA	GE
16	AR	AR	TA	TA	GE	GE	GE
17	AR	TA	TA	GE	GE	GE	CA
18	TA	TA	GE	GE	GE	CA	CA
19	TA	TA	GE	GE	CA	CA	CA
20	GE	GE	GE	CA	CA	CA	LE
21	GE	GE	CA	CA	CA	LE	LE
22	GE	CA	CA	CA	LE	LE	VI
23	CA	CA	CA	LE	LE	LE	VI
24	CA	CA	LE	LE	LE	VI	VI
25	CA	LE	LE	LE	VI	VI	LI
26	LE	LE	VI	VI	VI	LI	LI
27	LE	VI	VI	VI	LI	LI	SC
28	VI	VI	VI	LI	LI	LI	SC
29	VI	VI	LI	LI	LI	SC	SC

AR = Aries, TA = Taurus, GE = Gemini, CA = Cancer, LE = Leo, VI = Virgo, LI = Libra, SC = Scorpio, SA = Sagittarius, CP = Capricorn, AQ = Aquarius, PI = Pisces

MOON SIGNS

Moon in Aries

You have a strong imagination, courage, determination and a desire to do things in your own way and forge your own path through life.

Originality is a key attribute; you are seldom stuck for ideas although your mind is changeable and you could take the time to focus on individual tasks. Often quick-tempered, you take orders from few people and live life at a fast pace. Avoid health problems by taking regular time out for rest and relaxation.

Emotionally, it is important that you talk to those you are closest to and work out your true feelings. Once you discover that people are there to help, there is less necessity for you to do everything yourself.

Moon in Taurus

The Moon in Taurus gives you a courteous and friendly manner, which means you are likely to have many friends.

The good things in life mean a lot to you, as Taurus is an Earth sign that delights in experiences which please the senses. Hence you are probably a lover of good food and drink, which may in turn mean you need to keep an eye on the bathroom scales, especially as looking good is also important to you.

Emotionally you are fairly stable and you stick by your own standards. Taureans do not respond well to change. Intuition also plays an important part in your life.

Moon in Gemini

You have a warm-hearted character, sympathetic and eager to help others. At times reserved, you can also be articulate and chatty: this is part of the paradox of Gemini, which always brings duplicity to the nature. You are interested in current affairs, have a good intellect, and are good company and likely to have many friends. Most of your friends have a high opinion of you and would be ready to defend you should the need arise. However, this is usually unnecessary, as you are quite capable of defending yourself in any verbal confrontation.

Travel is important to your inquisitive mind and you find intellectual stimulus in mixing with people from different cultures. You also gain much from reading, writing and the arts but you do need plenty of rest and relaxation in order to avoid fatigue.

Moon in Cancer

The Moon in Cancer at the time of birth is a fortunate position as Cancer is the Moon's natural home. This means that the qualities of compassion and understanding given by the Moon are especially enhanced in your nature, and you are friendly and sociable and cope well with emotional pressures. You cherish home and family life, and happily do the domestic tasks. Your surroundings are important to you and you hate squalor and filth. You are likely to have a love of music and poetry.

Your basic character, although at times changeable like the Moon itself, depends on symmetry. You aim to make your surroundings comfortable and harmonious, for yourself and those close to you.

Moon in Leo

The best qualities of the Moon and Leo come together to make you warmhearted, fair, ambitious and self-confident. With good organisational abilities, you invariably rise to a position of responsibility in your chosen career. This is fortunate as you don't enjoy being an 'also-ran' and would rather be an important part of a small organisation than a menial in a large one.

You should be lucky in love, and happy, provided you put in the effort to make a comfortable home for yourself and those close to you. It is likely that you will have a love of pleasure, sport, music and literature. Life brings you many rewards, most of them as a direct result of your own efforts, although you may be luckier than average and ready to make the best of any situation.

Moon in Virgo

You are endowed with good mental abilities and a keen receptive memory, but you are never ostentatious or pretentious. Naturally quite reserved, you still have many friends, especially of the opposite sex. Marital relationships must be discussed carefully and worked at so that they remain harmonious, as personal attachments can be a problem if you do not give them your full attention.

Talented and persevering, you possess artistic qualities and are a good homemaker. Earning your honours through genuine merit, you work long and hard towards your objectives but show little pride in your achievements. Many short journeys will be undertaken in your life.

Moon in Libra

With the Moon in Libra you are naturally popular and make friends easily. People like you, probably more than you realise, you bring fun to a party and are a natural diplomat. For all its good points, Libra is not the most stable of astrological signs and, as a result, your emotions can be a little unstable too. Therefore, although the Moon in Libra is said to be good for love and marriage, your Sun sign and Rising sign will have an important effect on your emotional and loving qualities.

You must remember to relate to others in your decision-making. Co-operation is crucial because Libra represents the 'balance' of life that can only be achieved through harmonious relationships. Conformity is not easy for you because Libra, an Air sign, likes its independence.

Moon in Scorpio

Some people might call you pushy. In fact, all you really want to do is to live life to the full and protect yourself and your family from the pressures of life. Take care to avoid giving the impression of being sarcastic or impulsive and use your energies wisely and constructively.

You have great courage and you invariably achieve your goals by force of personality and sheer effort. You are fond of mystery and are good at predicting the outcome of situations and events. Travel experiences can be beneficial to you.

You may experience problems if you do not take time to examine your motives in a relationship, and also if you allow jealousy, always a feature of Scorpio, to cloud your judgement.

Moon in Sagittarius

The Moon in Sagittarius helps to make you a generous individual with humanitarian qualities and a kind heart. Restlessness may be intrinsic as your mind is seldom still. Perhaps because of this, you have a need for change that could lead you to several major moves during your adult life. You are not afraid to stand your ground when you know your judgement is right, you speak directly and have good intuition.

At work you are quick, efficient and versatile and so you make an ideal employee. You need work to be intellectually demanding and do not enjoy tedious routines.

In relationships, you anger quickly if faced with stupidity or deception, though you are just as quick to forgive and forget. Emotionally, there are times when your heart rules your head.

Moon in Capricorn

The Moon in Capricorn makes you popular and likely to come into the public eye in some way. The watery Moon is not entirely comfortable in the Earth sign of Capricorn and this may lead to some difficulties in the early years of life. An initial lack of creative ability and indecision must be overcome before the true qualities of patience and perseverance inherent in Capricorn can show through.

You have good administrative ability and are a capable worker, and if you are careful you can accumulate wealth. But you must be cautious and take professional advice in partnerships, as you are open to deception. You may be interested in social or welfare work, which suit your organisational skills and sympathy for others.

Moon in Aquarius

The Moon in Aquarius makes you an active and agreeable person with a friendly, easy-going nature. Sympathetic to the needs of others, you flourish in a laid-back atmosphere. You are broad-minded, fair and open to suggestion, although sometimes you have an unconventional quality which others can find hard to understand.

You are interested in the strange and curious, and in old articles and places. You enjoy trips to these places and gain much from them. Political, scientific and educational work interests you and you might choose a career in science or technology.

Money-wise, you make gains through innovation and concentration and Lunar Aquarians often tackle more than one job at a time. In love you are kind and honest.

Moon in Pisces

You have a kind, sympathetic nature, somewhat retiring at times, but you always take account of others' feelings and help when you can.

Personal relationships may be problematic, but as life goes on you can learn from your experiences and develop a better understanding of yourself and the world around you.

You have a fondness for travel, appreciate beauty and harmony and hate disorder and strife. You may be fond of literature and would make a good writer or speaker yourself. You have a creative imagination and may come across as an incurable romantic. You have strong intuition, maybe bordering on a mediumistic quality, which sets you apart from the mass. You may not be rich in cash terms, but your personal gifts are worth more than gold.

SCORPIO IN LOVE

Discover how compatible you are with people from the same and other parts of the zodiac. Five stars equals a match made in heaven!

Scorpio meets Scorpio

Scorpio is deep, complex and enigmatic, traits which often lead to misunderstanding with other zodiac signs, so a double Scorpio match can work well because both parties understand one another. They will allow each other periods of silence and reflection but still be willing to help, advise and support when necessary. Their relationship may seem odd to others but that doesn't matter if those involved are happy. All in all, an unusual but contented combination. Star rating: *****

Scorpio meets Sagittarius

Sagittarius needs constant stimulation and loves to be busy from dawn till dusk which may mean that it feels rather frustrated by Scorpio. Scorpions are hard workers, too, but they are also contemplative and need periods of quiet which may mean that they appear dull to Sagittarius. This could lead to a gulf between the two which must be overcome. With time and patience on both sides, this can be a lucrative encounter and good in terms of home and family. A variable alliance. Star rating: ***

Scorpio meets Capricorn

Lack of communication is the governing factor here. Neither of this pair are renowned communicators and both need a partner to draw out their full verbal potential. Consequently, Scorpio may find Capricorn cold and unapproachable while Capricorn could find Scorpio dark and brooding. Both are naturally tidy and would keep a pristine house but great effort and a mutual goal is needed on both sides to overcome the missing spark. A good match on the financial side, but probably not an earthshattering personal encounter. Star rating: **

Scorpio meets Aquarius

This is a promising and practical combination. Scorpio responds well to Aquarius' exploration of its deep nature and so this shy sign becomes lighter, brighter and more inspirational. Meanwhile, Aquarians are rarely as sure of themselves as they like to appear and are reassured by Scorpio's steady and determined support. Both signs want to be kind to the other which is a basis for a relationship that should be warm most of the time and extremely hot occasionally. Star rating: ****

Scorpio meets Pisces

If ever there were two zodiac signs that have a total rapport, it has to be Scorpio and Pisces. They share very similar needs: they are not gregarious and are happy with a little silence, good music and time to contemplate the finer things in life, and both are attracted to family life. Apart, they can have a tendency to wander in a romantic sense, but this is reduced when they come together. They are deep, firm friends who enjoy each other's company and this must lead to an excellent chance of success. These people are surely made for each other! Star rating: *****

Scorpio meets Aries

There can be great affection here, even if the two signs are so very different. The common link is the planet Mars, which plays a part in both these natures. Although Aries is, outwardly, the most dominant, Scorpio people are among the most powerful to be found anywhere. This quiet determination is respected by Aries. Aries will satisfy the passionate side of Scorpio, particularly with instruction from Scorpio. There are mysteries here which will add spice to life. The few arguments that do occur are likely to be awe-inspiring. Star rating: ****

Scorpio meets Taurus

Scorpio is deep – very deep – which may be a problem, because Taurus doesn't wear its heart on its sleeve either. It might be difficult for this pair to get together, because neither is naturally inclined to make the first move. Taurus stands in awe of the power and intensity of the Scorpio mind, while the Scorpion is interested in the Bull's affable and friendly qualities, so an enduring relationship could be forged if the couple ever get round to talking. Both are lovers of home and family, which will help to cement a relationship. Star rating: **

Scorpio meets Gemini

There could be problems here. Scorpio is one of the deepest and least understood of all the zodiac signs, which at first seems like a challenge to intellectual Gemini, who thinks it can solve anything. But the deeper the Gemini digs, the further down Scorpio goes. Meanwhile, Scorpio may be finding Gemini thoughtless, shallow and even downright annoying. Gemini is often afraid of Scorpio's perception and strength, together with the sting in the Scorpion's tail. Anything is possible, but the outlook for this match is less than promising. Star rating: **

Scorpio meets Cancer

This match is potentially a great success, a fact which is often a mystery to astrologers. Some feel it is due to the compatibility of the Water element, but it could also come from a mixture of similarity and difference in the personalities. Scorpio is partly ruled by Mars, which gives it a deep, passionate, dominant and powerful side. Cancerians generally like and respect this amalgam, and recognise something there that they would like to adopt themselves. On the other side of the coin, Scorpio needs love and emotional security which Cancer offers generously. Star rating: *****

Scorpio meets Leo

Stand back and watch the sparks fly! Scorpio has the deep sensitivity of a Water sign but it is also partially ruled by Fire planet Mars, from which it draws great power, and Leo will find that difficult. Leo loves to take charge and really hates to feel psychologically undermined, which is Scorpio's stock-in-trade. Scorpio may find Leo's ideals a little shallow, which will be upsetting to the Lion. Anything is possible, but this possibility is rather slimmer than most. Star rating: **

Scorpio meets Virgo

There are one or two potential difficulties here, but there is also a meeting point from which to overcome them. Virgo is very caring and protective, a trait which Scorpio understands and even emulates. Scorpio will impress Virgo with its serious side. Both signs are consistent, although also sarcastic. Scorpio may uncover a hidden passion in Virgo which all too often lies deep within its Earth-sign nature. Material success is very likely, with Virgo taking the lion's share of the domestic chores and family responsibilities. Star rating: ***

Scorpio meets Libra

Many astrologers have reservations about this match because, on the surface, the signs are so different. However, this couple may find fulfilment because these differences mean that their respective needs are met. Scorpio needs a partner to lighten the load, which won't daunt Libra, while Libra looks for a steadfast quality which it doesn't possess, but which Scorpio can supply naturally. Financial success is possible because they both have good ideas and back them up with hard work and determination. All in all, a promising outlook. Star rating: ****

VENUS: THE PLANET OF LOVE

If you look up at the sky around sunset or sunrise you will often see Venus in close attendance to the Sun. It is arguably one of the most beautiful sights of all and there is little wonder that historically it became associated with the goddess of love. But although Venus does play an important part in the way you view love and in the way others see you romantically, this is only one of the spheres of influence that it enjoys in your overall character.

Venus has a part to play in the more cultured side of your life and has much to do with your appreciation of art, literature, music and general creativity. Even the way you look is responsive to the part of the zodiac that Venus occupied at the start of your life, though this fact is also down to your Sun sign and Ascending sign. If, at the time you were born, Venus occupied one of the more gregarious zodiac signs, you will be more likely to wear your heart on your sleeve, as well as to be more attracted to entertainment, social gatherings and good company. If on the other hand Venus occupied a quiet zodiac sign at the time of your birth, you would tend to be more retiring and less willing to shine in public situations.

It's good to know what part the planet Venus plays in your life for it can have a great bearing on the way you appear to the rest of the world and since we all have to mix with others, you can learn to make the very best of what Venus has to offer you.

One of the great complications in the past has always been trying to establish exactly what zodiac position Venus enjoyed when you were born because the planet is notoriously difficult to track. However, I have solved that problem by creating a table that is exclusive to your Sun sign, which you will find on the following page.

Establishing your Venus sign could not be easier. Just look up the year of your birth on the page opposite and you will see a sign of the zodiac. This was the sign that Venus occupied in the period covered by your sign in that year. If Venus occupied more than one sign during the period, this is indicated by the date on which the sign changed, and the name of the new sign. For instance, if you were born in 1950, Venus was in Libra until the 28th October, after which time it was in Scorpio. If you were born before 28th October your Venus sign is Libra, if you were born on or after 28th October, your Venus sign is Scorpio. Once you have established the position of Venus at the time of your birth, you can then look in the pages which follow to see how this has a bearing on your life as a whole.

1915 SCORPIO / 9.11 SAGITTARIUS
1916 VIRGO / 3.11 LIBRA
1917 SAGITTARIUS / 7.11 CAPRICORN
1918 LIBRA / 30.10 SCORPIO
1919 VIRGO / 9.11 LIBRA
1920 SCORPIO / 24.10 SAGITTARIUS / 17.11 CAPRICORN
1921 LIBRA / 14.11 SCORPIO
1922 SAGITTARIUS / 16.11 SCORPIO
1923 SCORPIO / 9.11 SAGITTARIUS
1924 VIRGO / 3.11 LIBRA
1925 SAGITTARIUS / 7.11 CAPRICORN
1926 LIBRA / 29.10 SCORPIO
1927 VIRGO / 10.11 LIBRA
1928 SAGITTARIUS / 17.11 CAPRICORN
1929 LIBRA / 13.11 SCORPIO
1930 SAGITTARIUS / 16.11 SCORPIO
1931 SCORPIO / 8.11 SAGITTARIUS
1932 VIRGO / 2.11 LIBRA
1933 SAGITTARIUS / 7.11 CAPRICORN
1934 LIBRA / 29.10 SCORPIO
1935 VIRGO / 10.11 LIBRA
1936 SAGITTARIUS / 16.11 CAPRICORN
1937 LIBRA / 13.11 SCORPIO
1938 SAGITTARIUS / 16.11 SCORPIO
1939 SCORPIO / 7.11 SAGITTARIUS
1940 VIRGO / 2.11 LIBRA
1941 SAGITTARIUS / 7.11 CAPRICORN
1942 LIBRA / 28.10 SCORPIO
1943 VIRGO / 10.11 LIBRA
1944 SAGITTARIUS / 16.11 CAPRICORN
1945 LIBRA / 13.11 SCORPIO
1946 SAGITTARIUS / 16.11 SCORPIO
1947 SCORPIO / 6.11 SAGITTARIUS
1948 VIRGO / 1.11 LIBRA
1949 SAGITTARIUS / 6.11 CAPRICORN
1950 LIBRA / 28.10 SCORPIO
1951 VIRGO / 10.11 LIBRA
1952 SAGITTARIUS / 16.11 CAPRICORN
1953 LIBRA / 12.11 SCORPIO
1954 SAGITTARIUS / 28.10 SCORPIO
1955 SCORPIO / 6.11 SAGITTARIUS
1956 VIRGO / 1.11 LIBRA
1957 SAGITTARIUS / 6.11 CAPRICORN
1958 LIBRA / 27.10 SCORPIO
1959 VIRGO / 10.11 LIBRA
1960 SAGITTARIUS / 15.11 CAPRICORN
1961 LIBRA / 12.11 SCORPIO
1962 SAGITTARIUS / 28.10 SCORPIO
1963 SCORPIO / 5.11 SAGITTARIUS
1964 VIRGO / 31.10 LIBRA
1965 SAGITTARIUS / 6.11 CAPRICORN
1966 LIBRA / 27.10 SCORPIO
1967 VIRGO / 10.11 LIBRA
1968 SAGITTARIUS / 15.11 CAPRICORN
1969 LIBRA / 11.11 SCORPIO
1970 SAGITTARIUS / 28.10 SCORPIO
1971 SCORPIO / 4.11 SAGITTARIUS
1972 VIRGO / 31.10 LIBRA
1973 SAGITTARIUS / 6.11 CAPRICORN
1974 LIBRA / 26.10 SCORPIO
1975 VIRGO / 9.11 LIBRA
1976 SAGITTARIUS / 15.11 CAPRICORN
1977 LIBRA / 11.11 SCORPIO
1978 SAGITTARIUS / 28.10 SCORPIO
1979 SCORPIO / 4.11 SAGITTARIUS
1980 VIRGO / 30.10 LIBRA
1981 SAGITTARIUS / 5.11 CAPRICORN
1982 LIBRA / 26.10 SCORPIO
1983 VIRGO / 9.11 LIBRA
1984 SAGITTARIUS / 14.11 CAPRICORN
1985 LIBRA / 10.11 SCORPIO
1986 SAGITTARIUS / 28.10 SCORPIO
1987 SCORPIO / 3.11 SAGITTARIUS
1988 VIRGO / 30.10 LIBRA
1989 SAGITTARIUS / 5.11 CAPRICORN
1990 LIBRA / 25.10 SCORPIO
1991 VIRGO / 9.11 LIBRA
1992 SAGITTARIUS / 14.11 CAPRICORN
1993 LIBRA / 10.11 SCORPIO
1994 SAGITTARIUS / 28.10 SCORPIO
1995 SCORPIO / 3.11 SAGITTARIUS
1996 VIRGO / 29.10 LIBRA
1997 SAGITTARIUS / 5.11 CAPRICORN
1998 LIBRA / 25.10 SCORPIO
1999 VIRGO / 9.11 LIBRA
2000 SAGITTARIUS / 14.11 CAPRICORN
2001 LIBRA / 10.11 SCORPIO
2002 SAGITTARIUS / 28.10 SCORPIO
2003 SCORPIO / 3.11 SAGITTARIUS
2004 VIRGO / 29.10 LIBRA
2005 SAGITTARIUS / 5.11 CAPRICORN
2006 LIBRA / 25.10 SCORPIO
2007 VIRGO / 9.11 LIBRA
2008 SAGITTARIUS / 14.11 CAPRICORN
2009 LIBRA / 10.11 SCORPIO
2010 SAGITTARIUS / 28.10 SCORPIO
2011 SCORPIO / 3.11 SAGITTARIUS
2012 VIRGO / 29.10 LIBRA
2013 SAGITTARIUS / 5.11 CAPRICORN

VENUS THROUGH THE ZODIAC SIGNS

Venus in Aries

Amongst other things, the position of Venus in Aries indicates a fondness for travel, music and all creative pursuits. Your nature tends to be affectionate and you would try not to create confusion or difficulty for others if it could be avoided. Many people with this planetary position have a great love of the theatre, and mental stimulation is of the greatest importance. Early romantic attachments are common with Venus in Aries, so it is very important to establish a genuine sense of romantic continuity. Early marriage is not recommended, especially if it is based on sympathy. You may give your heart a little too readily on occasions.

Venus in Taurus

You are capable of very deep feelings and your emotions tend to last for a very long time. This makes you a trusting partner and lover, whose constancy is second to none. In life you are precise and careful and always try to do things the right way. Although this means an ordered life, which you are comfortable with, it can also lead you to be rather too fussy for your own good. Despite your pleasant nature, you are very fixed in your opinions and quite able to speak your mind. Others are attracted to you and historical astrologers always quoted this position of Venus as being very fortunate in terms of marriage. However, if you find yourself involved in a failed relationship, it could take you a long time to trust again.

Venus in Gemini

As with all associations related to Gemini, you tend to be quite versatile, anxious for change and intelligent in your dealings with the world at large. You may gain money from more than one source but you are equally good at spending it. There is an inference here that you are a good communicator, via either the written or the spoken word, and you love to be in the company of interesting people. Always on the look-out for culture, you may also be very fond of music, and love to indulge the curious and cultured side of your nature. In romance you tend to have more than one relationship and could find yourself associated with someone who has previously been a friend or even a distant relative.

Venus in Cancer

You often stay close to home because you are very fond of family and enjoy many of your most treasured moments when you are with those you love. Being naturally sympathetic, you will always do anything you can to support those around you, even people you hardly know at all. This charitable side of your nature is your most noticeable trait and is one of the reasons why others are naturally so fond of you. Being receptive and in some cases even psychic, you can see through to the soul of most of those with whom you come into contact. You may not commence too many romantic attachments but when you do give your heart, it tends to be unconditionally.

Venus in Leo

It must become quickly obvious to almost anyone you meet that you are kind, sympathetic and yet determined enough to stand up for anyone or anything that is truly important to you. Bright and sunny, you warm the world with your natural enthusiasm and would rarely do anything to hurt those around you, or at least not intentionally. In romance you are ardent and sincere, though some may find your style just a little overpowering. Gains come through your contacts with other people and this could be especially true with regard to romance, for love and money often come hand in hand for those who were born with Venus in Leo. People claim to understand you, though you are more complex than you seem.

Venus in Virgo

Your nature could well be fairly quiet no matter what your Sun sign might be, though this fact often manifests itself as an inner peace and would not prevent you from being basically sociable. Some delays and even the odd disappointment in love cannot be ruled out with this planetary position, though it's a fact that you will usually find the happiness you look for in the end. Catapulting yourself into romantic entanglements that you know to be rather ill-advised is not sensible, and it would be better to wait before you committed yourself exclusively to any one person. It is the essence of your nature to serve the world at large and through doing so it is possible that you will attract money at some stage in your life.

Venus in Libra

Venus is very comfortable in Libra and bestows upon those people who have this planetary position a particular sort of kindness that is easy to recognise. This is a very good position for all sorts of friendships and also for romantic attachments that usually bring much joy into your life. Few individuals with Venus in Libra would avoid marriage and since you are capable of great depths of love, it is likely that you will find a contented personal life. You like to mix with people of integrity and intelligence but don't take kindly to scruffy surroundings or work that means getting your hands too dirty. Careful speculation, good business dealings and money through marriage all seem fairly likely.

Venus in Scorpio

You are quite open and tend to spend money quite freely, even on those occasions when you don't have very much. Although your intentions are always good, there are times when you get yourself in to the odd scrape and this can be particularly true when it comes to romance, which you may come to late or from a rather unexpected direction. Certainly you have the power to be happy and to make others contented on the way, but you find the odd stumbling block on your journey through life and it could seem that you have to work harder than those around you. As a result of this, you gain a much deeper understanding of the true value of personal happiness than many people ever do, and are likely to achieve true contentment in the end.

Venus in Sagittarius

You are lighthearted, cheerful and always able to see the funny side of any situation. These facts enhance your popularity, which is especially high with members of the opposite sex. You should never have to look too far to find romantic interest in your life, though it is just possible that you might be too willing to commit yourself before you are certain that the person in question is right for you. Part of the problem here extends to other areas of life too. The fact is that you like variety in everything and so can tire of situations that fail to offer it. All the same, if you choose wisely and learn to understand your restless side, then great happiness can be yours.

Venus in Capricorn

The most notable trait that comes from Venus in this position is that it makes you trustworthy and able to take on all sorts of responsibilities in life. People are instinctively fond of you and love you all the more because you are always ready to help those who are in any form of need. Social and business popularity can be yours and there is a magnetic quality to your nature that is particularly attractive in a romantic sense. Anyone who wants a partner for a lover, a spouse and a good friend too would almost certainly look in your direction. Constancy is the hallmark of your nature and unfaithfulness would go right against the grain. You might sometimes be a little too trusting.

Venus in Aquarius

This location of Venus offers a fondness for travel and a desire to try out something new at every possible opportunity. You are extremely easy to get along with and tend to have many friends from varied backgrounds, classes and inclinations. You like to live a distinct sort of life and gain a great deal from moving about, both in a career sense and with regard to your home. It is not out of the question that you could form a romantic attachment to someone who comes from far away or be attracted to a person of a distinctly artistic and original nature. What you cannot stand is jealousy, for you have friends of both sexes and would want to keep things that way.

Venus in Pisces

The first thing people tend to notice about you is your wonderful, warm smile. Being very charitable by nature you will do anything to help others, even if you don't know them well. Much of your life may be spent sorting out situations for other people, but it is very important to feel that you are living for yourself too. In the main, you remain cheerful, and tend to be quite attractive to members of the opposite sex. Where romantic attachments are concerned, you could be drawn to people who are significantly older or younger than yourself or to someone with a unique career or point of view. It might be best for you to avoid marrying whilst you are still very young.

THE ASTRAL DIARY

HOW THE DIAGRAMS WORK

Through the picture diagrams in the Astral Diary I want to help you to plot your year. With them you can see where the positive and negative aspects will be found in each month. To make the most of them, all you have to do is remember where and when!

Let me show you how they work ...

THE MONTH AT A GLANCE

Just as there are twelve separate zodiac signs, so astrologers believe that each sign has twelve separate aspects to life. Each of the twelve segments relates to a different personal aspect. I list them all every month so that their meanings are always clear.

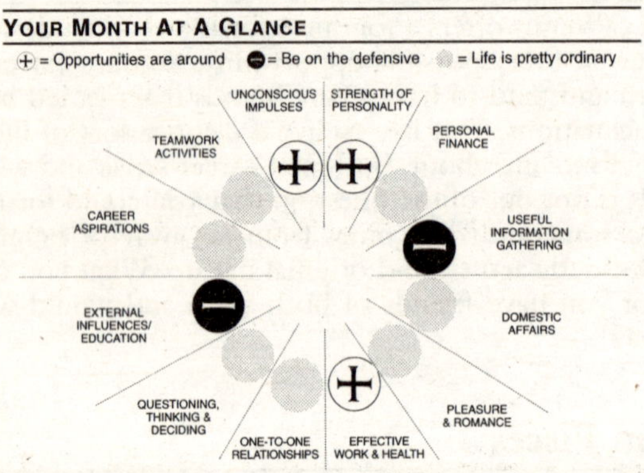

I have designed this chart to show you how and when these twelve different aspects are being influenced throughout the year. When there is a shaded circle, nothing out of the ordinary is to be expected. However, when a circle turns white with a plus sign, the influence is positive. Where the circle is black with a minus sign, it is a negative.

YOUR ENERGY RHYTHM CHART

On the opposite page is a picture diagram in which I link your zodiac group to the rhythm of the Moon. In doing this I have calculated when you will be gaining strength from its influence and equally when you may be weakened by it.

If you think of yourself as being like the tides of the ocean then you may understand how your own energies must also rise and fall. And if you understand how it works and when it is working, then you can better organise your activities to achieve more and get things done more easily.

YOUR ENERGY RHYTHM CHART

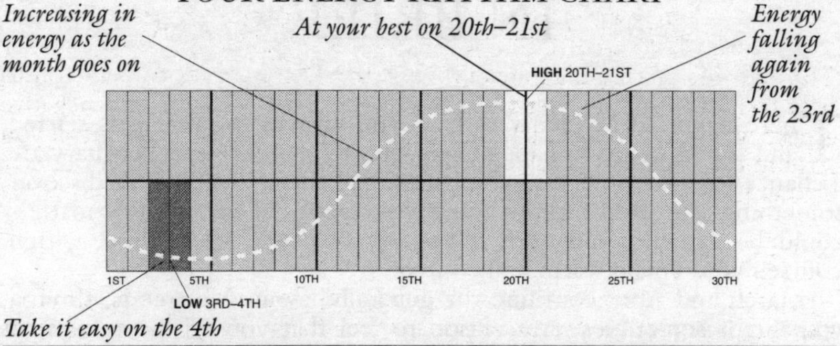

MOVING PICTURE SCREEN

Love, money, career and vitality measured every week

The diagram at the end of each week is designed to be informative and fun. The arrows move up and down the scale to give you an idea of the strength of your opportunities in each area. If LOVE stands at plus 4, then get out and put yourself about because things are going your way in romance! The further down the arrow goes, the weaker the opportunities. Do note that the diagram is an overall view of your astrological aspects and therefore reflects a trend which may not concur with every day in that cycle.

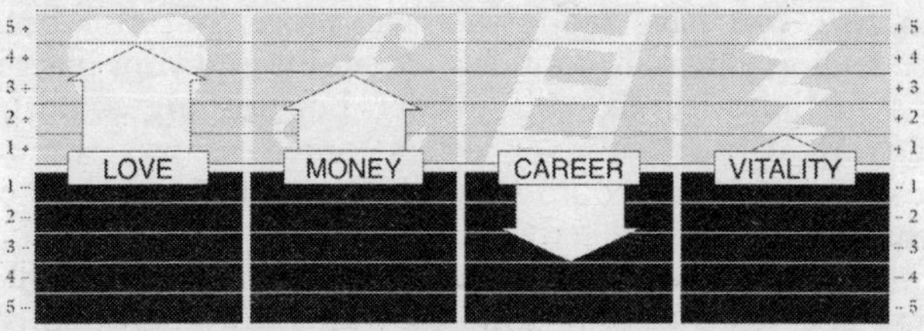

AND FINALLY:

am ....

pm ....

The two lines that are left blank in each daily entry of the Astral Diary are for your own personal use. You may find them ideal for keeping a check on birthdays or appointments, though it could also be an idea to make notes from the astrological trends and diagrams a few weeks in advance. Some of the lines are marked with a key, which indicates the working of astrological cycles in your life. Look out for them each week as they are the best days to take action or make decisions. The daily text tells you which area of your life to focus on.

☿ = Mercury is retrograde on that day.

SCORPIO: YOUR YEAR IN BRIEF

There ought to be plenty to keep you busy as the year gets started and things begin to happen very quickly. January and February are a chance to make progress in a professional sense, as well as to discover something you didn't know about your personal life. Money matters could be variable, and even if you are cold on the outside, within yourself you remain warm and content.

March and April continue the generally favourable trends, though you might sometimes have reason to feel that you are being slowed down by situations and influences that are beyond your own control. If you get on with jobs you don't want to do as quickly as you can, you will clear the decks for more positive trends and actions later. Some surprise visits may be in store and there are people entering your life who have much to teach you.

As the days lengthen and the weather gets warmer, so you tend to awaken from a sort of self-imposed hibernation. May and June will see you interacting much more with the world at large and getting out of the house on a more regular basis. There are gains to be made at work, as well as new things to learn that will enable you to feather your nest later. In terms of hobbies there is plenty to choose from at this time.

July and August are two of the best months for Scorpio during 2013, partly because you have scope to travel more, but also because you should be feeling generally confident about life and your place within it. You can sometimes feel like an outsider, but nothing could be further from the truth at this time. New offers come your way, some of which could be lucrative. You would be well advised to keep your eyes open during this period.

The year advances towards the autumn and you are still likely to be moving at a decent speed towards your most cherished objectives. September and October can be a mixed bag as far as personal attachments are concerned, and maybe you are not looking at relationships in a particularly sensible way. Financially speaking, there might be more money around than you had been expecting.

November and December should prove to be useful and heart-warming in a number of different ways. New friendships become possible and you are fully committed to changes both in and outside your home. You won't make much allowance for the winter weather that starts to descend, and you could still be travelling more than usual. Christmas-time should be happy and active and the New Year promises more of the same in terms of general forward progress.

January

2013

Your Month at a Glance

(+) = Opportunities are around (–) = Be on the defensive (●) = Life is pretty ordinary

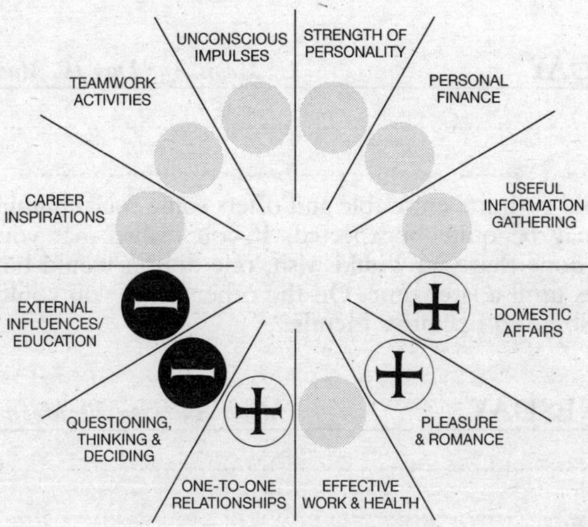

January Highs and Lows

Here I show you how the rhythms of the Moon will affect you this month. Like the tide, your energies and abilities will rise and fall with its pattern. When it is above the centre line, go for it, when it is below, you should be resting.

31 MONDAY *Moon Age Day 18 Moon Sign Leo*

am ....

pm ....

If you make sure you recognise the needs of those around you, it is possible to get everything fully on course for an evening that everyone can enjoy. All the same, you need to be aware of any slight problems in your love life. Although this reminds you that you have to show that extra bit of concern and love, it shouldn't be a lasting situation.

1 TUESDAY *Moon Age Day 19 Moon Sign Leo*

am ....

pm ....

Today should be quite enjoyable and offers some social highlights, some of which may be quite unexpected. If you realise that you can't get everything done that you would wish, one option would be to delay a few routines until a later time. On the other hand, you could enlist the support of some co-operative friends.

2 WEDNESDAY *Moon Age Day 20 Moon Sign Virgo*

am ....

pm ....

At the beginning of today it's worth recognising that a lucky streak is hard to find, although this would have been quite useful at the moment. As the day wears on things should change. The position of the Moon could certainly allow you to undertake a rethink regarding specific relationships and the way you view them.

3 THURSDAY *Moon Age Day 21 Moon Sign Virgo*

am ....

pm ....

Discussions and negotiations about what you see as vital issues might not take others in quite the same way. Patience is the key in such situations, and you needn't allow the more brooding side of your Scorpio nature to get in the way of objectivity. Remember that people lead busy lives and sometimes don't think enough.

4 FRIDAY *Moon Age Day 22 Moon Sign Virgo*

am..

pm..

Your powers to attract the better things in life certainly seem to be improving now. This has potential to be a busy Friday, but one that can work to your advantage. If there appears to be nothing ahead but work and worry, you really are not looking at the positive side of life as much as you should.

5 SATURDAY *Moon Age Day 23 Moon Sign Libra*

am..

pm..

The spotlight is now on the acquisition of money, and you are encouraged to turn your mind to this today. Whether your earning power is growing substantially, or you're thinking about taking on new and more rewarding responsibilities, there are good reasons to devote some time to looking over your personal finances.

6 SUNDAY *Moon Age Day 24 Moon Sign Libra*

am..

pm..

The ups and downs of the Scorpio nature could be surfacing more today than has been the case for a week or two. Bear in mind that others might see this as moodiness, whereas you would merely describe yourself as 'pensive'. Either way you will need to make that extra effort in order to show that you are ready to talk freely.

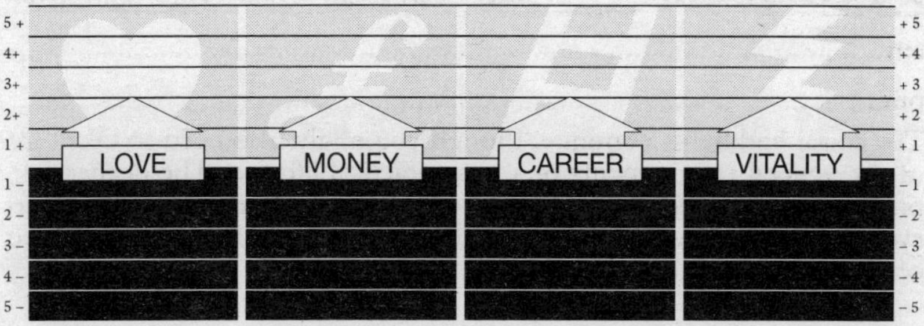

7 MONDAY *Moon Age Day 25 Moon Sign Scorpio*

am ....

pm ....

As the lunar high arrives, you have everything you need to keep several different projects on the go at the same time. Your best approach is not to rush your fences and, if necessary, to leave some of the routine tasks until later. What's really important today is to do whatever you undertake to the best of your ability.

8 TUESDAY *Moon Age Day 26 Moon Sign Scorpio*

am ....

pm ....

This is an excellent time to put in that extra bit of effort. New incentives are well marked, and you have what it takes to keep up a hectic and exciting social life. Any form of sport has a great deal to offer you right now, though you still need to find the time to show loved ones how much you care about them.

9 WEDNESDAY *Moon Age Day 27 Moon Sign Sagittarius*

am ....

pm ....

There are signs that you want everything you can get from life – and you want it now! The world should look good from a Scorpio perspective at this time, and you have scope to get on very well in practical terms too. A Scorpio this bright is a force to be reckoned with, and you shouldn't have any trouble turning heads.

10 THURSDAY *Moon Age Day 28 Moon Sign Sagittarius*

am ....

pm ....

The social highlights continue, though you might also need to take care of the general requirements of a busy practical life too. The deeper side of your nature puts in an appearance, keeping busy should help you to avoid any dark thoughts. Even if confidence isn't lacking, it may well be of an unusual sort.

11 FRIDAY *Moon Age Day 29 Moon Sign Capricorn*

am..

pm..

Money-making endeavours are well highlighted and you should discover that you have the knack of getting things right at this stage of the week. If you make the most of the luck that is available, you can finish the working week with a flourish. You have a chance to make the weekend quite exciting – starting from this evening!

12 SATURDAY *Moon Age Day 0 Moon Sign Capricorn*

am..

pm..

You can afford to push forward today, particularly in terms of communication. It's a question of making sure that others are really listening to you, and that they have your best interests at heart. Even if you aren't too keen to commit yourself to financial speculation at present, there's nothing wrong with looking at a suggestion.

13 SUNDAY *Moon Age Day 1 Moon Sign Aquarius*

am..

pm..

Whether or not you are at work today, it's possible that professional issues might seem more trouble than they are worth. Rather than blowing them up out of all proportion, you would be wise to simply leave them alone. With plenty to play for in the relationship stakes, it's time to tell people how you feel.

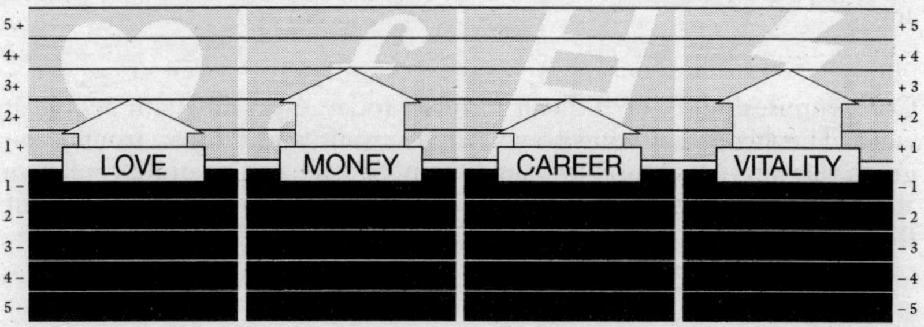

14 MONDAY *Moon Age Day 2 Moon Sign Aquarius*

am ....

pm ....

You can still impress others, and in most areas of your life. It's natural for attitudes to vary within your friendship circle, and you can't expect to agree with everyone's point of view. Neither can you rely on diplomacy. The time has come to give a truthful answer to any question you are asked.

15 TUESDAY *Moon Age Day 3 Moon Sign Pisces*

am ....

pm ....

The message today is to get busy and to stay that way for most of the day. If this isn't possible, you may simply have to make some attempt to look as though you are doing something important. This is especially true at work, where it's vital to demonstrate your capacity to get things done, particularly to superiors.

16 WEDNESDAY *Moon Age Day 4 Moon Sign Pisces*

am ....

pm ....

You are now in a position to take full advantage of practical situations. You have an opportunity to get things done at home, and seem to have a particularly good ability to organise and arrange things. All in all, this could well be a busy day, but one during which you should be working to your full potential.

17 THURSDAY *Moon Age Day 5 Moon Sign Aries*

am ....

pm ....

Compromises might be difficult to make today, especially with people at work. The fact is that you know what you want, and if those around you get in the way, it's natural to blame them. Scorpio can be quite vindictive and even a little destructive on occasions. You need to ensure you are not that way now.

18 FRIDAY *Moon Age Day 6 Moon Sign Aries*

am ....

pm..

A favourable period for personal and communication matters. It's a question of using the odd trick you have up your sleeve in order to get ahead of the herd. This is an excellent time for all sporting activities, or for taking a journey that has been planned only hours ahead. Confidence is present when you know what you are doing.

19 SATURDAY *Moon Age Day 7 Moon Sign Aries*

am ....

pm..

You could now feel that your influence on life is decreasing somewhat. This needn't matter too much, particularly if you feel happy to rest and relax. Getting those little personal chores out of the way can bring you great satisfaction, and by the end of the day you might simply decide to lounge in a hot bath!

20 SUNDAY *Moon Age Day 8 Moon Sign Taurus*

am ....

pm..

Although you don't need to give in to the lunar low, it does little to help the level of energy you have available. Why not settle for a stay-at-home sort of Sunday during which you don't have to push yourself personally? After all, this isn't a time of year that lends itself to getting very much done in any case.

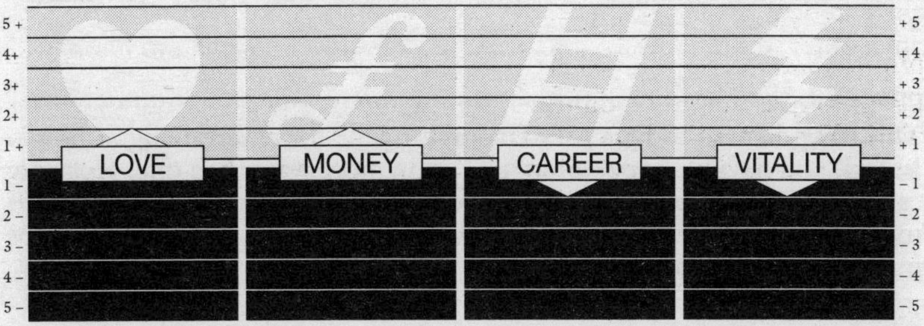

21 MONDAY *Moon Age Day 9 Moon Sign Taurus*

am..

pm..

A lull is in place, and there may not be a great deal you can do about it. Your best approach is to pursue quiet activities and spend time with family members. As long as you are not champing at the bit to get on with jobs that simply can't be done, there is no reason why this has to be a particularly unlucky or difficult day.

22 TUESDAY *Moon Age Day 10 Moon Sign Gemini*

am..

pm..

The Sun enters your solar fourth house, bringing a new trend that is positive for all matters related to your home and family. This would be an ideal time to build bridges with anyone who has proved difficult in the recent past, and to ensure that intimate relationships are less strained than of late.

23 WEDNESDAY *Moon Age Day 11 Moon Sign Gemini*

am..

pm..

Even if you are very busy at the moment, this fact needn't prevent you from taking even more on. There are good reasons to count your blessings, and that should help you to remain generally cheerful, even on the odd occasion when things go wrong. Your patience over a particular issue can make all the difference.

24 THURSDAY *Moon Age Day 12 Moon Sign Gemini*

am..

pm..

This has potential to be a very favourable time for entertaining at home. In fact, you have an opportunity to gain in more ways than one. Not only can you enjoy the purely domestic side of the day, you can also find ways to extend the benefits to business or social contacts. Organised groups might play a part in your thinking.

25 FRIDAY *Moon Age Day 13 Moon Sign Cancer*

am..

pm..

There ought to be plenty of time for fun and games, some of a deeply personal nature. A winter holiday would suit you down to the ground at this time, but if you can't get one, you could at least spend some time away from everyday routines. Planning some weekend shopping could work wonders.

26 SATURDAY *Moon Age Day 14 Moon Sign Cancer*

am..

pm..

At the moment, making progress means being in the know. That is why it pays to keep your eyes and ears open. The more you pay attention to what is happening around you, the greater is your chance of keeping up. This is particularly true for working Scorpio people who hold significant responsibility.

27 SUNDAY *Moon Age Day 15 Moon Sign Leo*

am..

pm..

Your current pace of activity shows no signs at all of slowing. Remember that you are only human and, if necessary, force yourself into a way of living that allows time for rest and reflection. One approach would be to look at your routines and itemise those jobs that could easily wait until later.

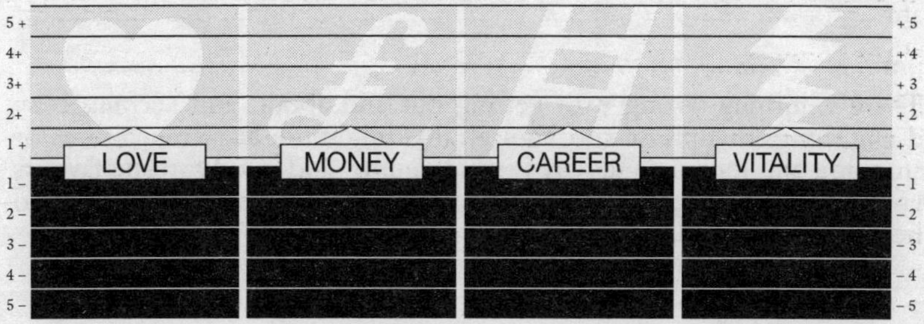

28 MONDAY *Moon Age Day 16 Moon Sign Leo*

am ....

pm ....

Be prepared to deal with any strong disagreements that crop up today. Such a state of affairs is more likely if those around you insist on being right all the time. For your own part, the position of Mars in your chart now highlights the stubborn side of your nature. Are you willing to admit that you could be wrong?

29 TUESDAY *Moon Age Day 17 Moon Sign Virgo*

am ....

pm ....

Trends indicate a need to broaden your horizons, which could include taking the opportunity to travel more this year. You can start to investigate the possibilities of doing so almost immediately, in terms of planning, if not in reality. Take a broad view of potentials, particularly your own.

30 WEDNESDAY *Moon Age Day 18 Moon Sign Virgo*

am ....

pm ....

This looks like a great time to explore local scenery. True, it is the middle of winter, but that shouldn't bother anyone born under the sign of Scorpio. A little fresh air would probably do you good, and blowing away the cobwebs can help you to think far more clearly. Pleasing your friends is also the order of the day.

31 THURSDAY *Moon Age Day 19 Moon Sign Virgo*

am ....

pm ....

There's nothing wrong with getting out and about, and keeping busy doing things that please you, though that might not leave much time for stopping and looking. Activity is what counts, and good fortune favours your efforts once again. Avoid arguments at home, which are unlikely to help your case at all.

1 FRIDAY *Moon Age Day 20 Moon Sign Libra*

am ....

pm ....

The first day of February has potential to be one of the best days possible for family gatherings. Even if you don't choose to travel about at this time, it's worth trying to surround yourself with the people you love. The sense of nostalgia continues, assisting you to make the best of this family-minded interlude.

2 SATURDAY *Moon Age Day 21 Moon Sign Libra*

am ....

pm ....

Be ready to increase the pace of everyday life dramatically, to avoid being left out in the cold when there are gains to be made. All the same, this is a day for planning, rather than one for specifically doing. Tomorrow comes soon enough, when the Moon enters your zodiac sign. For the moment, it pays to look ahead.

3 SUNDAY *Moon Age Day 22 Moon Sign Scorpio*

am ....

pm ....

The lunar high emphasises your clear determination to get your own way. That doesn't mean you have to forget about the needs of others. On the contrary, for every success you make, you are in a position to make sure that plenty of other people benefit too. It's time to get Lady Luck on your side and give her all the help you can.

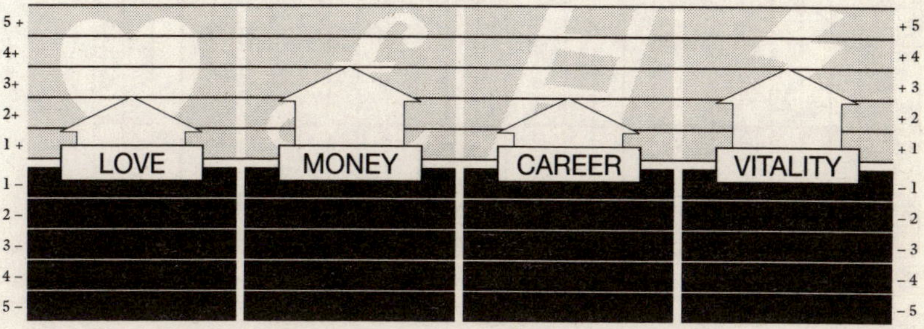

February

2013

Your Month at a Glance

(+) = Opportunities are around (−) = Be on the defensive (●) = Life is pretty ordinary

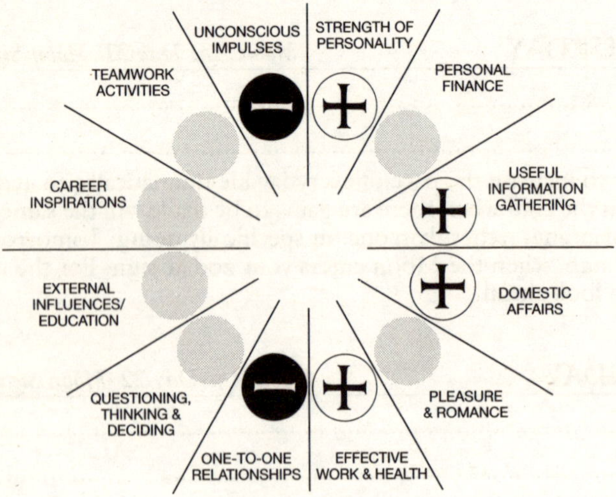

February Highs and Lows

Here I show you how the rhythms of the Moon will affect you this month. Like the tide, your energies and abilities will rise and fall with its pattern. When it is above the centre line, go for it, when it is below, you should be resting.

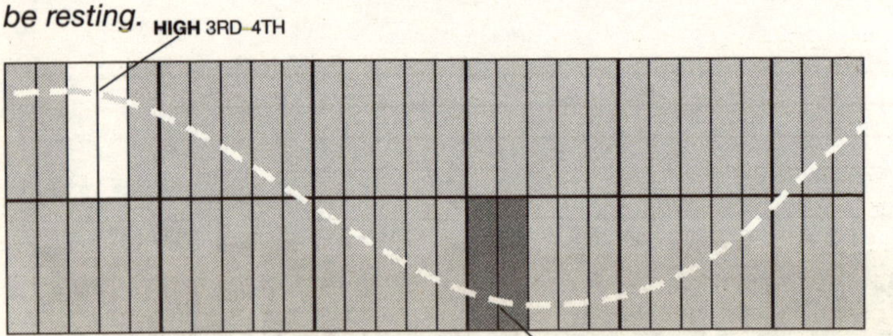

4 MONDAY *Moon Age Day 23 Moon Sign Scorpio*

am ....

pm ....

This is a day during which you can capitalise on some positive influences in the material sphere. It could even feel as though things are more or less automatically coming your way as and when you need them. Seeking assistance from others can certainly help with this. Your affectionate side is to the fore now.

5 TUESDAY *Moon Age Day 24 Moon Sign Sagittarius*

am ....

pm ....

You can gain a great deal from friendly assistance, and from being willing to do what others ask of you. This is a social day and one that helps you to discover how much you are loved and respected by others. Even if you remain friendly and generally interested, it might still be hard to do more than one thing at once.

6 WEDNESDAY *Moon Age Day 25 Moon Sign Sagittarius*

am ....

pm ....

Be ready to respond to criticism of your ideas and opinions. Since this is part of a planetary process that leads towards advancement, it is important that you see things in this light. Try not to get annoyed if you are being asked questions that seem to test your resolve. It's up to you to come up with some answers.

7 THURSDAY *Moon Age Day 26 Moon Sign Capricorn*

am ....

pm ....

Along comes a potentially hectic phase during which you will need to keep abreast of news and views. It's a question of keeping busy on many different fronts, while at the same time doing your best to support those family members who have specific needs right now. A degree of organisation is vital!

8 FRIDAY *Moon Age Day 27 Moon Sign Capricorn*

am ....

pm ....

This might be a good time for a change of scene. Why not get away from the everyday routines and find some way to enjoy yourself, if only for a few hours? All work and no play makes anyone dull, and particularly Scorpio today. Vitality and enthusiasm are heightened when you are genuinely interested in life.

9 SATURDAY *Moon Age Day 28 Moon Sign Aquarius*

am ....

pm ....

Do you feel that others are subtly trying to manipulate your ideas at this time? It's really important that you make up your own mind now and that you do not allow yourself to be directed down avenues that you know are not for you. If this means being stubborn, then that's how you will have to be.

10 SUNDAY *Moon Age Day 0 Moon Sign Aquarius*

am ....

pm ....

An uplift in your general spirits regarding work is now likely, possibly as a result of actions you took yesterday. Keep up your efforts when it comes to getting your message across to other people. The spotlight is also on general health issues, and if you can make improvements in this area, so much the better.

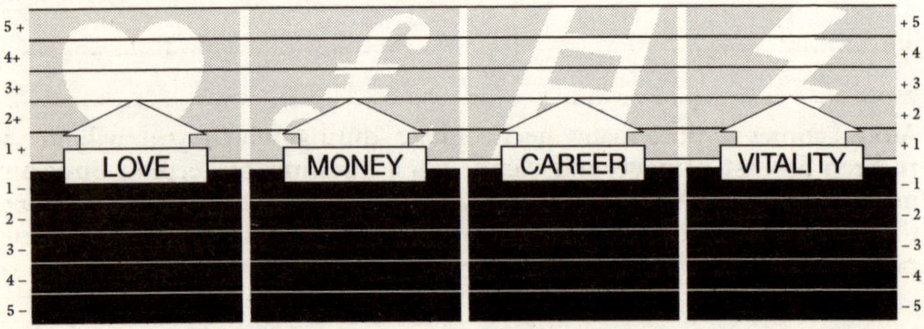

11 MONDAY *Moon Age Day 1 Moon Sign Pisces*

am...

pm...

Take advantage of a boost at work and with regard to all practical matters. You can't expect everything to be going your way at the moment, but should be focusing on those issues that matter the most. Any sort of research that you are planning to undertake would be particularly well accented at this time.

12 TUESDAY *Moon Age Day 2 Moon Sign Pisces*

am...

pm...

This is a period when enjoying simply being yourself is the name of the game. If any difficulties arise in terms of the way in which your nature has a bearing on other people, you need to explain yourself to them. You won't get very far if you begin altering your basic characteristics simply to please the world at large.

13 WEDNESDAY *Moon Age Day 3 Moon Sign Pisces*

am...

pm...

There is a continued lively accent on social mixing, especially with people you know and like a great deal. It's time to commit yourself to deep, personal attachments and to be willing to tell people what you really think. When it comes to important meetings, there's nothing at all wrong with speaking your mind.

14 THURSDAY *Moon Age Day 4 Moon Sign Aries*

am...

pm...

Love life and romance count for a great deal now. At the same time there should be opportunities to enjoy entertainments of various sorts. Your imagination is emphasised, suggesting that a visit to the theatre or a cinema would appeal. Whatever you decide to do today, it's important not to push yourself too hard.

15 FRIDAY *Moon Age Day 5 Moon Sign Aries*

am...

pm...

Are professional matters going less smoothly than you would wish? Acting on instinct could make all the difference, and there is less emphasis on showing the practical side of your nature. It's important not to rush your fences. Be willing to spend quality time with people you like.

16 SATURDAY *Moon Age Day 6 Moon Sign Taurus*

am...

pm...

Even if you are willing enough to be of assistance and to do what you can for almost anyone, your ability to offer practical help may be limited today, thanks to the presence of the lunar low. This is a time when it might be difficult to find the motivation that has been present recently, and a period during which you need to think.

17 SUNDAY *Moon Age Day 7 Moon Sign Taurus*

am...

pm...

Another day on which your spirits and enthusiasm could be rather low. Once again you have to understand that this short-term trend can be used in a positive way. Trying to overturn obstacles now merely means wasting energy. Instead, watch and wait. By tomorrow prospects are improved and you can get yourself back on form.

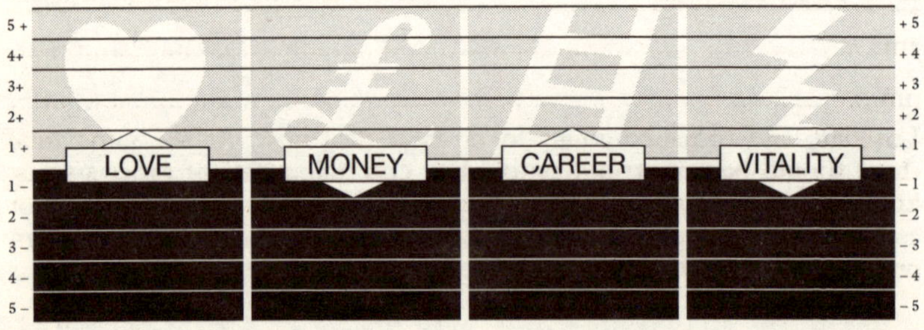

18 MONDAY *Moon Age Day 8 Moon Sign Gemini*

am ....

pm ....

You have scope to get the most from pleasure and leisure pursuits, and may be in the mood for some luxury. Scorpio people are capable of really spoiling themselves, and today could be such an opportunity. Just remember that it's best to tackle any practical jobs first, and that time is important at the moment.

19 TUESDAY *Moon Age Day 9 Moon Sign Gemini*

am ....

pm ....

Confidence is the order of the day at present, and should assist you to make short work of the sort of tasks that sometimes make you feel apprehensive. Be prepared to offer help to family members who need support now. Any slight selfishness that was in evidence earlier can now be put to one side.

20 WEDNESDAY *Moon Age Day 10 Moon Sign Gemini*

am ....

pm ....

This has potential to be one of the better days of the month when it comes to getting what you want from life generally. Avoiding a tendency to be argumentative should help, as will your refusal to rise to any bait that is offered. Allow artistic pursuits to capture your imagination, especially in home-based projects.

21 THURSDAY *Moon Age Day 11 Moon Sign Cancer*

am ....

pm ....

Trends suggest that happiness is now to be found in the company of close friends, though the confidence you feel in public settings may not be at its highest. What does remain absolutely intact is your sense of humour, which could easily see you through any potentially embarrassing situations.

22 FRIDAY *Moon Age Day 12 Moon Sign Cancer*

am ....

pm ....

It might now be more difficult to come up with new ideas than was the case earlier in the month. Be willing to think things through carefully and avoid rushing your fences. That little green-eyed god jealousy is never far from the surface, but you needn't allow yourself to be possessed by him at this time.

23 SATURDAY ☿ *Moon Age Day 13 Moon Sign Leo*

am ....

pm ....

A favourable period for all domestic matters is clearly available to you now. You can use this to achieve closeness in family relationships, and can also offer help and advice to others. Don't be too willing to spill all the beans. There are some things that are best left unsaid, no matter how much pressure you come under.

24 SUNDAY ☿ *Moon Age Day 14 Moon Sign Leo*

am ....

pm ....

Be ready to deal with any disputes that occur in relationships, though if you can prevent them occurring in the first place, so much the better! Don't put off until tomorrow any task you can do today, and make sure you get an early start on what you need to do. You may not like the prospect, but it should pay off.

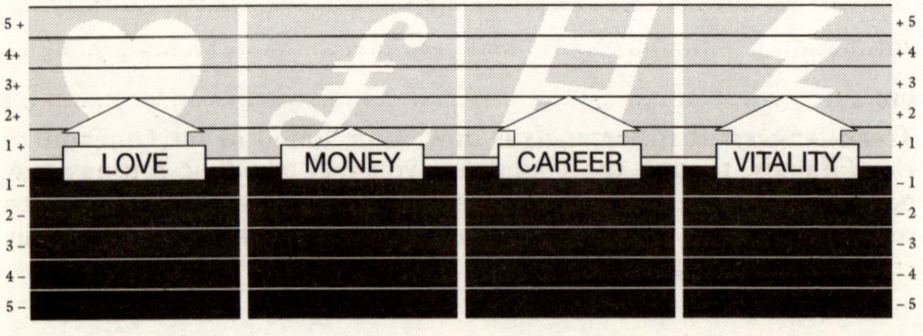

25 MONDAY ☿ *Moon Age Day 15 Moon Sign Leo*

am..

pm..

This can be a socially uplifting day, with much to set it apart and the chance to get ahead in the career stakes. You can afford to take things at face value, and certainly needn't doubt your own capabilities. Concern for the underdog is highlighted now, a sure sign that your more sympathetic qualities are to the fore.

26 TUESDAY ☿ *Moon Age Day 16 Moon Sign Virgo*

am..

pm..

It pays to keep self-righteous behaviour under lock and key, because you don't have any time for it at present. Today is about fulfilling your own expectations, so it's obvious what a negative attitude is likely to achieve. By all means stick to what you know at work, but be willing to try something new in your social life.

27 WEDNESDAY ☿ *Moon Age Day 17 Moon Sign Virgo*

am..

pm..

Creative efforts are well marked, so why not spend time doing something interesting at home? It's worth keeping your personal life to yourself for the moment, and don't let others in on your secrets. Financial issues are a different matter, and there is much to be said for talking things through with your partner or a family member.

28 THURSDAY ☿ *Moon Age Day 18 Moon Sign Libra*

am..

pm..

There is potential for career matters to go slightly off course, and it is particularly important for you to keep your eye on the ball at present. Ensuring that others don't get the better of you is fine, though this will mean that any problems that occur are probably self-created. Romantically speaking, you seem to be on the up.

1 FRIDAY ☿ *Moon Age Day 19 Moon Sign Libra*

am ....

pm ....

A day to act with determination, particularly if you think you are being watched. It isn't the weekend yet, and you might need to put in quite a lot of effort ahead of Saturday. There is much to be said for finding ways to enjoy yourself once the working day is over, maybe in the company of good friends.

2 SATURDAY ☿ *Moon Age Day 20 Moon Sign Scorpio*

am ....

pm ....

Be prepared to capitalise on all the opportunities that are available to you now that the lunar high has arrived. These have a definite bearing on the lives of working Scorpios, though you can also use them to a degree in your home life too. Finances can be strengthened, and this could leave you with slightly more flexibility.

3 SUNDAY ☿ *Moon Age Day 21 Moon Sign Scorpio*

am ....

pm ....

Take advantage of a day for getting ahead and a time when you simply have to snap your fingers in order to have your heart's desire. If you don't manage to make progress right now, you probably are not putting in quite the amount of effort necessary. The support you may be able to elicit from friends can make all the difference.

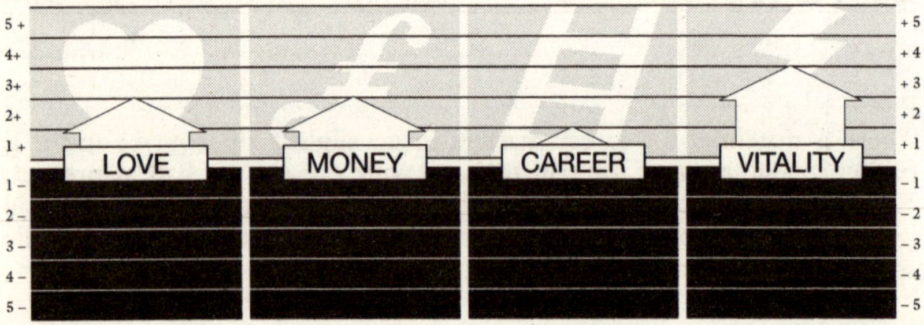

March

2013

Your Month at a Glance

(+) = Opportunities are around (−) = Be on the defensive (●) = Life is pretty ordinary

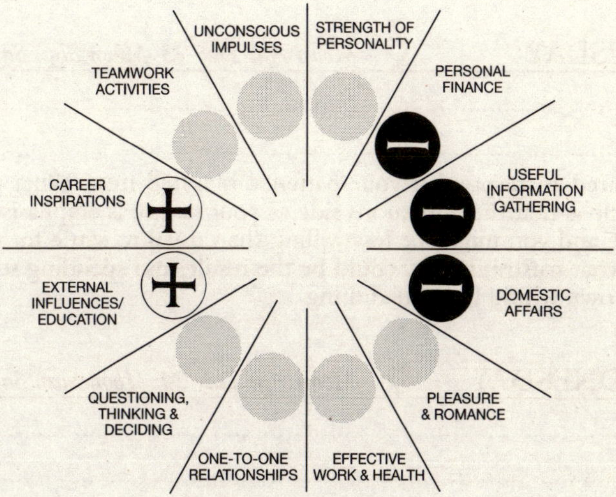

March Highs and Lows

Here I show you how the rhythms of the Moon will affect you this month. Like the tide, your energies and abilities will rise and fall with its pattern. When it is above the centre line, go for it, when it is below, you should be resting.

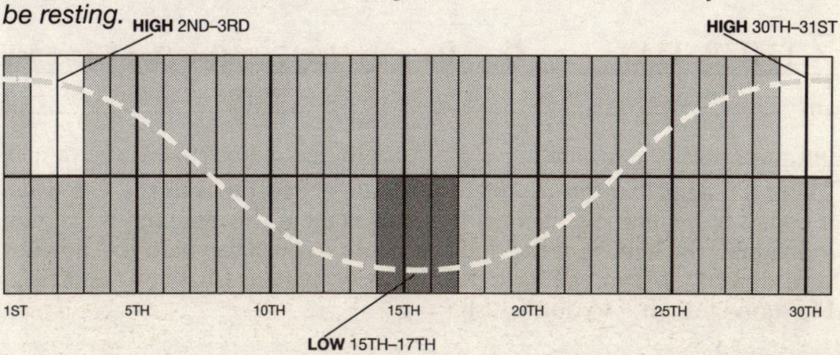

4 MONDAY ☿ *Moon Age Day 22 Moon Sign Sagittarius*

am..

pm..

This is a good time to be around your favourite people. You can gain a great deal simply from being in the company of those you like, which could well extend to specific family members. Try to avoid listening to gossip at the moment. It is entirely possible that you will get hold of the wrong end of the stick.

5 TUESDAY ☿ *Moon Age Day 23 Moon Sign Sagittarius*

am..

pm..

Be prepared to respond if your patience is tested now. What probably won't help is that the impetuous side of your nature is emphasised at the moment, and you might be less willing than usual to settle for routines. A somewhat frustrating day could be the result, and spending some time on your own would be no bad thing.

6 WEDNESDAY ☿ *Moon Age Day 24 Moon Sign Sagittarius*

am..

pm..

Though in a career sense you may notice new possibilities in the offing, your love life could easily seem less than satisfying. Perhaps the problem is being caused by you? It is worth taking a look at your general attitude and forcing a degree of flexibility to come into your general patterns of thinking.

7 THURSDAY ☿ *Moon Age Day 25 Moon Sign Capricorn*

am..

pm..

There are signs that the argumentative side of Scorpio is to the fore when it comes to general discussions. It is important at this time to give certain individuals the benefit of the doubt and not to push too hard to gain your own objectives. You will have the chance to pursue what you want from life soon enough – so don't rush.

8 FRIDAY ☿ *Moon Age Day 26 Moon Sign Capricorn*

am ....

pm ....

Career-wise it appears that you are in a risk-taking mood. That's fine, as long as your gambles are genuinely calculated ones. Conforming to expectations may not be too easy at present, and it is important to stretch yourself in some way. Plan now to make the coming weekend an exciting one.

9 SATURDAY ☿ *Moon Age Day 27 Moon Sign Aquarius*

am ....

pm ....

The Sun in its present position gives you every encouragement to let your light shine brightly today. Go for excitement if you can, and for mixing with people you find to be especially stimulating. Intersperse the genuine needs of the day with periods during which you simply set out to have a good time.

10 SUNDAY ☿ *Moon Age Day 28 Moon Sign Aquarius*

am ....

pm ....

Your sense of self-importance is highlighted, to the extent that you might expect it to be reflected in the way others are behaving towards you. Being at the heart of things does come naturally at the moment, particularly if you are insisting that those around you take notice.

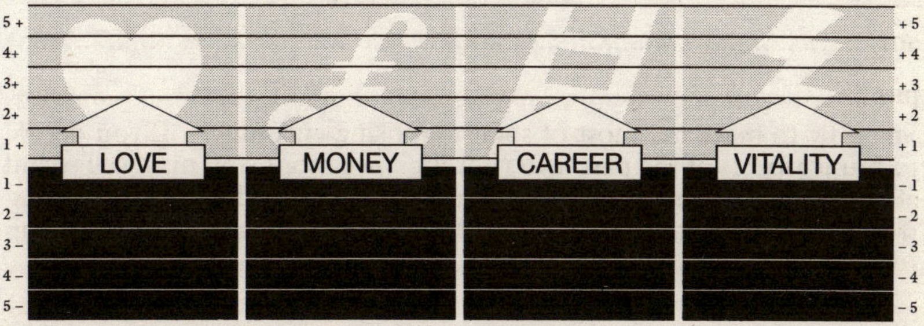

11 MONDAY ☿ *Moon Age Day 29 Moon Sign Pisces*

am ....

pm ....

Times change quickly and you can now afford to make having fun your number one priority. This might include spending time with like-minded people, and young Scorpio individuals especially could be burning the candle at both ends. Try to do something new and interesting on as many occasions today as you can.

12 TUESDAY ☿ *Moon Age Day 0 Moon Sign Pisces*

am ....

pm ....

You now have what it takes to make most areas of work and leisure run like a dream. With your conversational skills well accented, and plenty to play for, the sky really is the limit. It pays to let the darker side of the Scorpio nature take a holiday now, and discover how just how many people want to be your friend!

13 WEDNESDAY ☿ *Moon Age Day 1 Moon Sign Aries*

am ....

pm ....

You get the best from life now if you mix and mingle with as many different people as you can. Be ready to deal with any problems that arise in relation to specific arrangements, but in the main you can be funny, easy to talk to and great to have around. If words of love are on offer later on, believe what is being said.

14 THURSDAY ☿ *Moon Age Day 2 Moon Sign Aries*

am ....

pm ....

Stand by to make the most of some surprising encounters. If you decide to bring aspects of the past into your life once more, you may well spend almost as much time looking back as you do forwards. It's been a long slog to get to some of your objectives, but you should be able to reap some of the benefits soon.

15 FRIDAY ☿ *Moon Age Day 3 Moon Sign Taurus*

am ....

pm ....

A wind-down period is on offer, thanks to the arrival of the lunar low. You needn't allow it to have too much of a bearing on your life, unless you decide that you are going to try to move mountains. Why not leave all important plans for another day and be content to sit and watch life go by for a few hours?

16 SATURDAY ☿ *Moon Age Day 4 Moon Sign Taurus*

am ....

pm ....

The lunar low probably might mean settling for second-best, or at least that's the way things will look at first. As long as you are aware that this is a good time for relaxation, you can make the most of the day. Tomorrow you can start to leave behind the slightly negative influences, but for the moment you needn't push yourself.

17 SUNDAY ☿ *Moon Age Day 5 Moon Sign Taurus*

am ....

pm ....

As the Moon starts to move away from your opposite sign, it's time to show the world what you are made of. The opportunities to do so come thick and fast, and it pays to be as flexible and easy-going as you can. You have what it takes to attract compliments from all sorts of directions. Definitely not a stay-at-home Sunday!

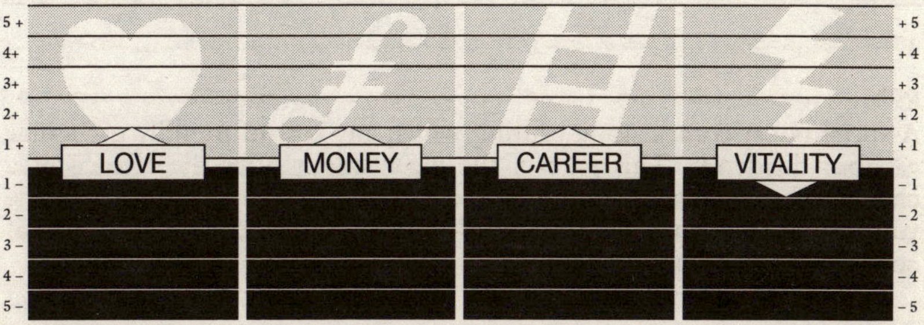

18 MONDAY ☿ *Moon Age Day 6 Moon Sign Gemini*

am ....

pm ....

A greater sense of control prevails now, and you may decide to slow things down. There are good reasons to tell certain people how you feel, and you have scope to do that today. By all means give yourself a pat on the back for a recent success, though beware of getting too complacent. There is still plenty to be achieved.

19 TUESDAY *Moon Age Day 7 Moon Sign Gemini*

am ....

pm ....

Personal co-operation with co-workers offers potential for good results today, so it's worth making sure you know what others are doing. Away from work, it's time to make sure that any minor problems within the family have been put right. This should help you create a happier home life and plenty of laughs.

20 WEDNESDAY *Moon Age Day 8 Moon Sign Cancer*

am ....

pm ....

The positive part that Venus has to play in your life should be quite obvious, particularly in professional relationships. Getting onside with the people who count should be easy enough, but you might have to show a good deal of compassion when it comes to your social life, particularly with friends.

21 THURSDAY *Moon Age Day 9 Moon Sign Cancer*

am ....

pm ....

A social boost comes along, during which any sort of friendly gathering can pay dividends. This part of the week might offer the chance of a change of scene, and even if you don't consider it to be spring just yet, you should gain from being out of doors. A long walk through beautiful countryside can work wonders.

22 FRIDAY *Moon Age Day 10 Moon Sign Cancer*

am ....

pm ....

Today is about being footloose and fancy-free, and in just the right frame of mind to get what you want. You are unlikely to achieve this objective by being difficult or pushy. On the contrary, you need to be sweetness itself, and willing to do as many good favours as there are hours in the day.

23 SATURDAY *Moon Age Day 11 Moon Sign Leo*

am ....

pm ....

Be prepared to deal with some disagreeable types around now. Although showing a civil attitude works best, that doesn't necessarily mean you have to like the people in question. What won't help today is losing your temper. This is a time when it is necessary to count to ten – more than once if necessary!

24 SUNDAY *Moon Age Day 12 Moon Sign Leo*

am ....

pm ....

You should find much to keep you reassured about life today, particularly behind closed doors and when you are in the company of your partner or lover. This is an ideal time to show the sensual side of your nature, and to enjoy the response you can attract. Practical matters could be fraught with potential problems.

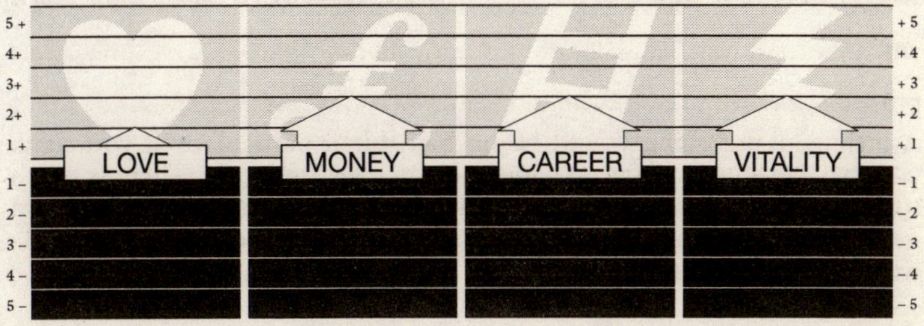

25 MONDAY *Moon Age Day 13 Moon Sign Virgo*

am ....

pm ....

You can help yourself to get by today by using your personal magnetism, which is well accented. Any disruption in work matters needn't matter too much if you are determined to dedicate most of today to having fun. An ideal time to plan holidays, or if you are especially lucky, to take a break from the late winter weather.

26 TUESDAY *Moon Age Day 14 Moon Sign Virgo*

am ....

pm ....

You can take almost any aspect of life in your stride today. Even if this isn't the most interesting part of the month, there are potential gains to be made. How the week turns out depends entirely on you. Most planetary trends are neutral, allowing a good deal of leeway and plenty of scope for you to create good times.

27 WEDNESDAY *Moon Age Day 15 Moon Sign Libra*

am ....

pm ....

You can happily tap into the help and support that you can elicit from the direction of others today. Instead of struggling with matters you are not able to resolve, it pays to turn to someone who has more experience than you do. Conversation, even at a casual level, could well carry some vital information now.

28 THURSDAY *Moon Age Day 16 Moon Sign Libra*

am ....

pm ....

A little soul-searching would be no bad thing, particularly if you think you may have been unfair to someone you care for deeply. There is much to be said for coming clean and making a full confession. You can then get on with enjoying yourself, especially if you are surrounded by people with a positive attitude.

29 FRIDAY *Moon Age Day 17 Moon Sign Libra*

am ....

pm ....

If you can slow down the pace of life, so much the better. The Moon is in your solar twelfth house, which always happens a day or two before the lunar high. You need to think and to plan, though you should avoid putting any of your wilder schemes into operation, at least until the middle of next week.

30 SATURDAY *Moon Age Day 18 Moon Sign Scorpio*

am ....

pm ....

Trends now assist you to get situations turning out more or less as you would wish. The lunar high offers better luck and an ability for you to use what comes your way more completely. You needn't be too concerned about rules and regulations – after all, they probably just get on your nerves!

31 SUNDAY *Moon Age Day 19 Moon Sign Scorpio*

am ....

pm ....

Freedom is the most important consideration today. Being restricted in any way is unlikely to suit you, and a kind of personal claustrophobia could well be the result if you are restrained by any circumstance. Your best response is to seek some wide open spaces and good fresh air throughout most of this Sunday.

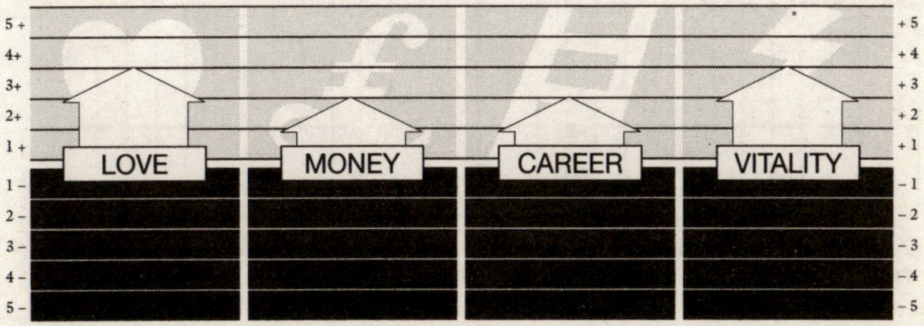

April

2013

Your Month at a Glance

(+) = Opportunities are around ⊖ = Be on the defensive ● = Life is pretty ordinary

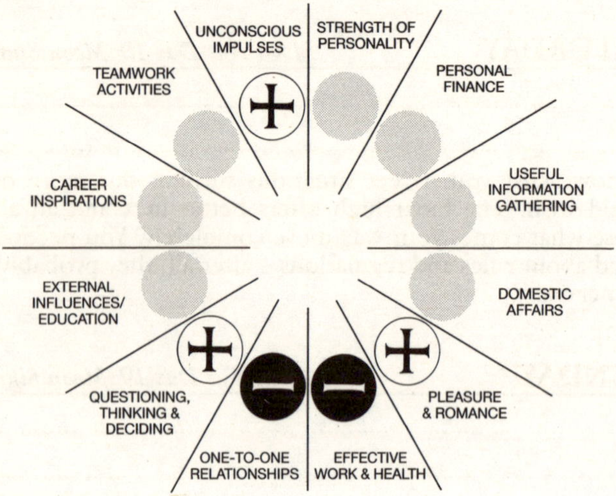

April Highs and Lows

Here I show you how the rhythms of the Moon will affect you this month. Like the tide, your energies and abilities will rise and fall with its pattern. When it is above the centre line, go for it, when it is below, you should be resting.

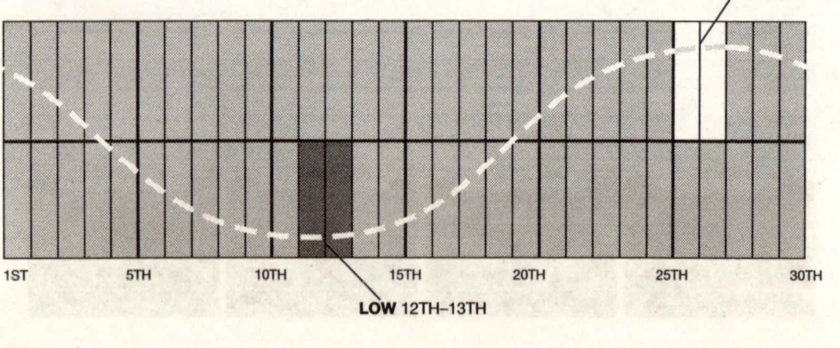

1 MONDAY *Moon Age Day 20 Moon Sign Sagittarius*

am ....

pm ....

You have scope to make the first day of April a pleasant one, even if it isn't particularly stimulating. If things have been going your way in the recent past, you might now feel that the roller-coaster ride is slowing down. There's nothing wrong with making the most of a lull in proceedings, so why not enjoy a break?

2 TUESDAY *Moon Age Day 21 Moon Sign Sagittarius*

am ....

pm ....

Considerable improvements are now possible in your working life if you are willing to put in the effort. Personal relationships may offer warmth and you may even be able to achieve a slightly better financial situation. Overall, this has potential to be a positive time and one during which contentment is within your reach.

3 WEDNESDAY *Moon Age Day 22 Moon Sign Capricorn*

am ....

pm ....

The pursuit of personal freedom can offer you the chance of happiness today. It's natural to feel uncomfortable if you are forced down paths that are not of your own choosing. Give and take in romantic attachments is another key to success at present, so be willing to look at an alternative point of view.

4 THURSDAY *Moon Age Day 23 Moon Sign Capricorn*

am ....

pm ....

You have what it takes to attract some warm responses from a host of people, not least those individuals you care for deeply. Young Scorpios, or those who have been actively looking for love, can make romantic progress at present. However, you need to be prepared to make some of the running yourself.

5 FRIDAY *Moon Age Day 24 Moon Sign Aquarius*

am ....

pm ....

This Friday offers a chance to create many light-hearted moments, plus the opportunity to look ahead and make some interesting plans for the weekend. Work hard today and make your time your own tomorrow. You may also decide to clear the working decks for even more action next week.

6 SATURDAY *Moon Age Day 25 Moon Sign Aquarius*

am ....

pm ....

It's true that you can be rather full of yourself today, but it's possible that you do get on better in general when you show a degree of self-confidence. Striking a sensible balance between the two situations might not be very easy, though you should be capable of showing a more modest side if you really try.

7 SUNDAY *Moon Age Day 26 Moon Sign Pisces*

am ....

pm ....

Today is about bringing out all the interesting elements in your social life. You can allow your curiosity to be roused over many different issues, and that makes you interested – and interesting! It's worth gathering friends around you at this time and finding out what fascinating news they have to impart.

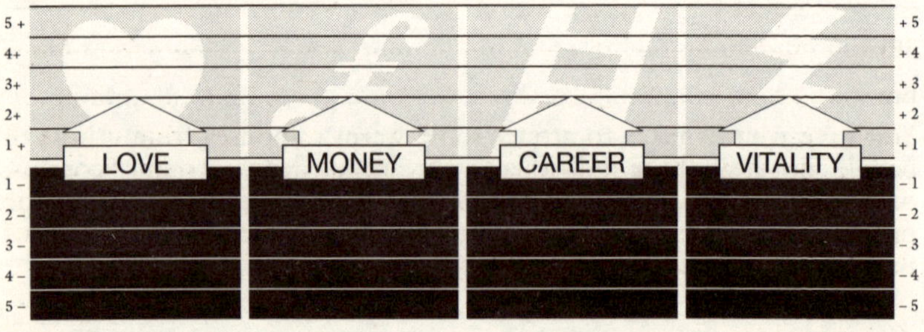

8 MONDAY *Moon Age Day 27 Moon Sign Pisces*

am ....

pm ....

Harmonious influences now surround you, and especially so with regard to love and romance. Trends assist you to be very approachable at this time and to show the most loving side of your Scorpio nature. This might also make you rather protective – perhaps a little too much so in some cases.

9 TUESDAY *Moon Age Day 28 Moon Sign Aries*

am ....

pm ....

In terms of your career you need to be ready to deal with minor setbacks at the moment. You need to ask yourself whether these are of any real importance. Don't be afraid to abandon something completely if you know you can then make a fresh start. A day to put any hesitancy to one side and be dynamic.

10 WEDNESDAY *Moon Age Day 0 Moon Sign Aries*

am ....

pm ....

Today the emphasis on fun continues. The same influences that highlight your social inclinations also make this an ideal time to show the more romantic side of your nature. Your best place today is among friends in places of entertainment. What is much less likely to appeal today is endless work, so take a break if you can.

11 THURSDAY *Moon Age Day 1 Moon Sign Aries*

am ....

pm ....

Although your mind is sharp at present, there's a danger you might speak without thinking. Be careful that you don't unintentionally offer offence. Scorpio people can be quite sarcastic on occasions, a quality of your nature that needs to be controlled. However, you can at least ensure your dealings with loved ones are pleasant.

12 FRIDAY *Moon Age Day 2 Moon Sign Taurus*

am ....

pm ....

An emotional issue or two can help you to recognise that your judgement may be somewhat clouded. You can thank the present position of the Moon for this. Do you feel you are lacking in confidence now? You need to realise that this is probably only in your head, and for all real purposes you can manage just fine.

13 SATURDAY *Moon Age Day 3 Moon Sign Taurus*

am ....

pm ....

The lunar low is still around, though it ought to prove to be less of a problem today. For one thing your strongly social side has returned, making it easier for you to get on with people at all levels. Spend at least part of today researching something. The effort should do you good, and can be quite productive.

14 SUNDAY *Moon Age Day 4 Moon Sign Gemini*

am ....

pm ....

It shouldn't be hard to find a warm welcome wherever you choose to go today. The weekend strengthens your social impulses and gives you every encouragement to mix with other people. Spending long periods on your own is not to be recommended at present, and neither is sulking if things don't go your way!

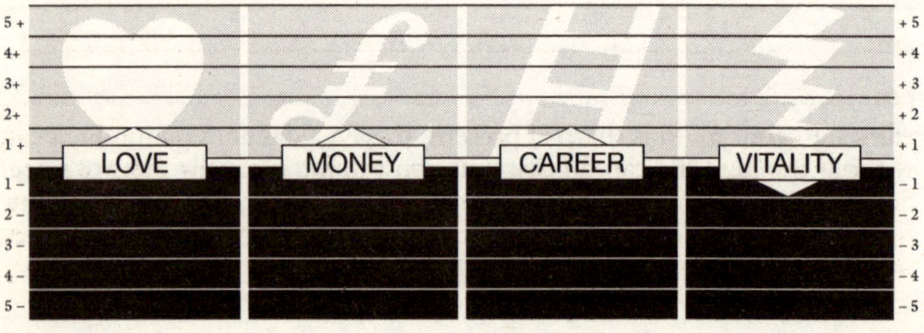

15 MONDAY *Moon Age Day 5 Moon Sign Gemini*

am ....

pm ....

This is a good period for twosomes, since personal attachments should be easier to deal with today. The same aspects promote the possibility of forging a close link with someone at work, and mixing business with pleasure is part of what today is about. Patience is the key when dealing with the insecurities of others.

16 TUESDAY *Moon Age Day 6 Moon Sign Gemini*

am ....

pm ....

Strong feelings can often lead to harsh words, and this is something you need to avoid today. Scorpio is going through a slightly antagonistic phase. On the rare occasions that this happens, the person who is most injured in the end is you. Better by far today to bite your tongue, rather than say something you will regret later.

17 WEDNESDAY *Moon Age Day 7 Moon Sign Cancer*

am ....

pm ....

Although a slightly uncooperative tendency is still in evidence, the placement of Mercury in your chart can help you to create some interesting and stimulating encounters. It's a question of meeting fresh individuals and even making new friends. You also might decide to bring people from the past back into your life.

18 THURSDAY *Moon Age Day 8 Moon Sign Cancer*

am ....

pm ....

Beware of falling foul of others in discussions today. Arguing is not to be recommended under current influences, and your best approach is to keep quiet rather than to say something you will regret later. You can't expect everyone to be on your side, but in any case you need first and foremost to rely on your own resources.

19 FRIDAY *Moon Age Day 9 Moon Sign Leo*

am ....

pm ....

At an emotional level a calmer view is now possible, and this should help you to see situations in their true light. It pays to get ahead of yourself at work, which should leave time free later to do what you want. If you don't have to commit yourself professionally ahead of the weekend, you can afford to find ways to really enjoy yourself.

20 SATURDAY *Moon Age Day 10 Moon Sign Leo*

am ....

pm ....

Social matters should help you to keep up your spirits today, but the best times are on offer just around the corner. If there is anything you want to do, plan to get cracking tomorrow. For the moment, it's worth seeking out the company of people you care about and avoiding doing more than you have to in a practical sense.

21 SUNDAY *Moon Age Day 11 Moon Sign Leo*

am ....

pm ....

Emotional involvements can offer you a great deal of satisfaction, even if this appears less than likely at the start of this Sunday. Why not opt for a change of scene or even a few hours at the shops? Trends suggest this is more likely to appeal to you than having to undertake tasks that really go against the grain.

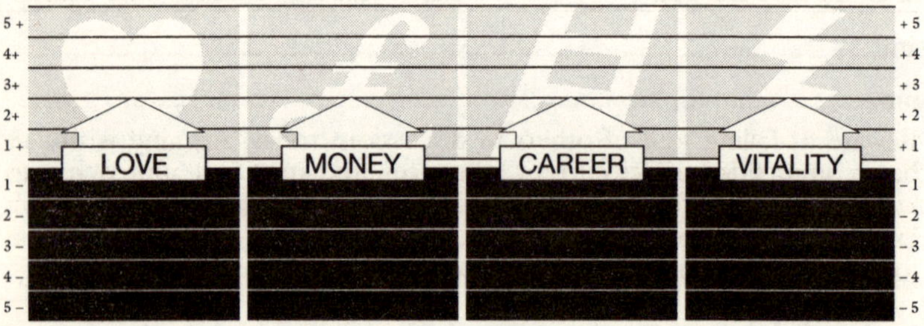

22 MONDAY *Moon Age Day 12 Moon Sign Virgo*

am..

pm..

Emotions could be close to the surface, especially if you are dealing with people whose attitudes and expectations are very different from yours. It would be sensible to take some time out, to simply recharge your batteries. In a social sense, sticking with people you both know and like is what today is all about.

23 TUESDAY *Moon Age Day 13 Moon Sign Virgo*

am..

pm..

Expectations in the professional sphere are emphasised, encouraging you to get ahead if opportunities present themselves. It's natural to feel concern for family members who seem to be having problems. However, it would be sensible to take a second look before committing yourself to drastic action.

24 WEDNESDAY *Moon Age Day 14 Moon Sign Libra*

am..

pm..

There might be a temptation to scatter your energies more than is necessary at present. It would be better by far to concentrate on one or two really important tasks and to leave other jobs until another day. When you can't tackle something yourself, it pays to look for someone else who can.

25 THURSDAY *Moon Age Day 15 Moon Sign Libra*

am..

pm..

You have scope to take your social life up a notch again, and with the Sun in your solar seventh house, you can make sure it's all go! It's time to pick up the pace of life, particularly if you've had a quiet time in recent days. Make sure that you know exactly what is expected of you before you commence any new projects.

26 FRIDAY *Moon Age Day 16 Moon Sign Scorpio*

am ....

pm ....

Make the most of the luck that is available as the lunar high pays you its April visit. Be willing to go where the action is and take on new projects at this time. Your ability to deal with even awkward people is emphasised right now, and you should find that the force of your personality is paying great dividends.

27 SATURDAY *Moon Age Day 17 Moon Sign Scorpio*

am ....

pm ....

This is the second day in a row during which the Moon in your zodiac sign can offer you a bundle of opportunities. Keep an open mind about proposed changes, particularly with regard to your working life. Some of the things you want are within your grasp right now, particularly if you are willing to ask for them.

28 SUNDAY *Moon Age Day 18 Moon Sign Sagittarius*

am ....

pm ....

Relationships can sometimes throw up the odd challenge and make it difficult for you to see the path ahead clearly. It's up to you to deal with any problems that arise now, and preferably to tackle them one at a time. Beware of biting off more than you can reasonably chew in any respect.

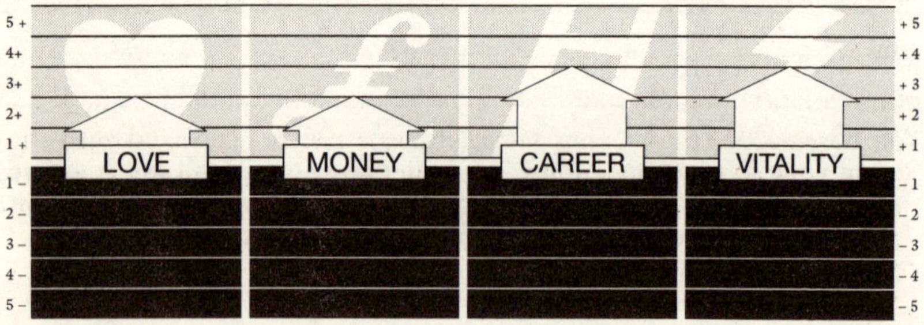

29 MONDAY *Moon Age Day 19 Moon Sign Sagittarius*

am ....

pm ....

Now that the Sun has moved on in your chart, you have a chance to get rid of any obstacles to success and happiness that have dogged you during the last three or four weeks. This has potential to be a very unusual period, but it's none the worse for that. As a Scorpion, you can easily cope with 'odd'.

30 TUESDAY *Moon Age Day 20 Moon Sign Capricorn*

am ....

pm ....

Matters at work can be progressed more quickly today than you might have been expecting. A very proactive approach works best today. Don't follow issues, but make them. You might even be able to catch people off their guard if they're not expecting you to utilise such a high level of executive ability.

1 WEDNESDAY *Moon Age Day 21 Moon Sign Capricorn*

am ....

pm ....

The first day of May is a chance to make great efforts to maintain a happy family life, perhaps somewhat against the odds. Younger people especially might be difficult to deal with, and there's a danger that you'll lose your temper. Although there is rarely any gain to be made by arguing, it might be unavoidable now.

2 THURSDAY *Moon Age Day 22 Moon Sign Aquarius*

am ....

pm ....

Be prepared to deal with a few precarious emotional issues today. Try not to react too strongly if others are behaving in what you see as being an irrational way. Remember that from their point of view, you are also acting strangely! All that is required is a little patience all round.

3 FRIDAY *Moon Age Day 23 Moon Sign Aquarius*

am ....

pm...

Trends suggest you may be focusing on matters from the past today, and a trip down memory lane is a possibility. Of course this is quite natural for Scorpio on occasions, but you should try to avoid being too captivated by events from long ago. Right now it would be better to set your sights on the future.

4 SATURDAY *Moon Age Day 24 Moon Sign Pisces*

am ....

pm...

Relationships can prove to be extremely helpful in a variety of different ways. Social encounters might be especially enjoyable, and should allow you to come up with a wealth of new ideas. From a financial perspective, the current interlude would be an ideal time to strengthen your position.

5 SUNDAY *Moon Age Day 25 Moon Sign Pisces*

am ....

pm...

Even if you now feel slightly less in control of your own life than you would wish, relinquishing a little of the control would probably be no bad thing. You need to find people who would be only too happy to have you rely on them. This, in turn, might actually prove to be of benefit for their own sense of well-being.

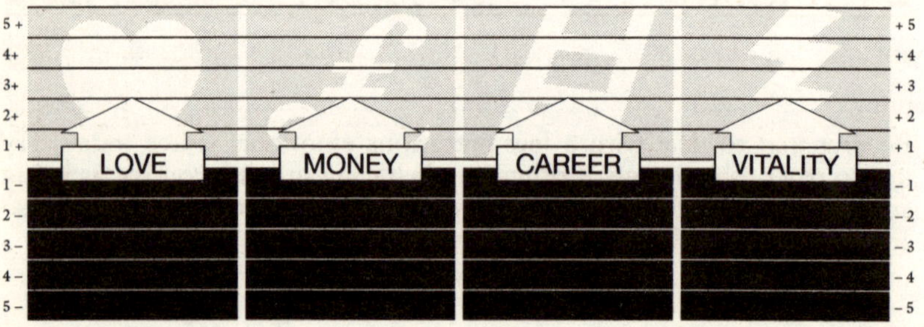

May 2013

Your Month at a Glance

⊕ = Opportunities are around ⊖ = Be on the defensive ● = Life is pretty ordinary

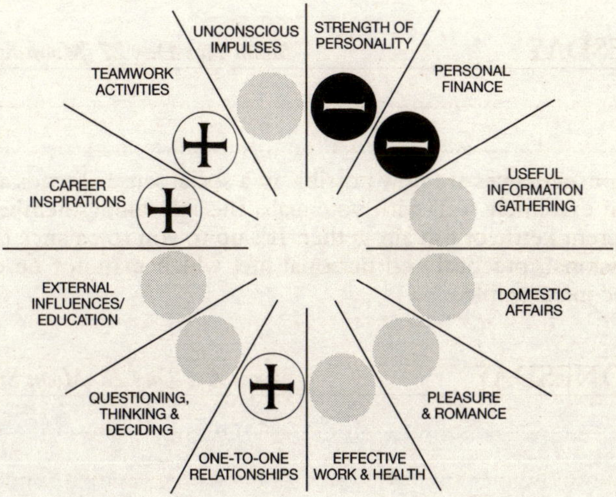

May Highs and Lows

Here I show you how the rhythms of the Moon will affect you this month. Like the tide, your energies and abilities will rise and fall with its pattern. When it is above the centre line, go for it, when it is below, you should be resting.

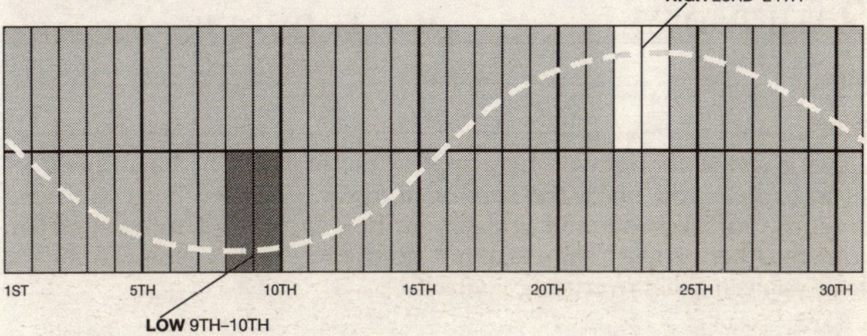

6 MONDAY *Moon Age Day 26 Moon Sign Pisces*

am ....

pm ....

By all means assert your ideas to others at home, though this might be less easy out there in the wider world. It might be tricky to get through to people who think about life very differently you. Allowing those around you the right to be themselves is imperative, but bear in mind that you can't necessarily emulate them.

7 TUESDAY *Moon Age Day 27 Moon Sign Aries*

am ....

pm ....

Uplifting experiences are now possible in a social sense. Trends assist you to get on extremely well with your pals, though family members could be a different kettle of fish altogether. It's up to you to balance the needs of professional, practical and personal life, which may not be easy, but should be manageable.

8 WEDNESDAY *Moon Age Day 28 Moon Sign Aries*

am ....

pm ....

Even if the relationships you are pursuing today don't seem to be as interesting as the ones you experienced yesterday, they could prove to be far more use in a practical sense. You also have what it takes to get on well with members of your family, even awkward ones who have caused you problems of late.

9 THURSDAY *Moon Age Day 29 Moon Sign Taurus*

am ....

pm ....

Does it feel as though you have applied the brakes? The lunar low does little to help you make the sort of headway you have been achieving recently. For Thursday and Friday, your best approach is to leave certain jobs to other people. They may not do them as well as you can, but at least you can avoid overtiring yourself.

10 FRIDAY *Moon Age Day 0 Moon Sign Taurus*

am ....

pm ....

Once again, enthusiasm may be hard to find as the lunar low continues. If you can't find sufficient energy, it will be difficult to move forward quite as positively as has been the case recently. Your best approach is to understand the way you are feeling and remain generally quiet, at least until the Moon has moved on.

11 SATURDAY *Moon Age Day 1 Moon Sign Gemini*

am ....

pm ....

The spotlight is now on career matters for many Scorpio people, though it's also important to find time to enjoy the social highlights that are available in your life today. Why not take an hour or two to do something that specifically pleases you? You needn't be in too much of a rush to volunteer for onerous tasks.

12 SUNDAY *Moon Age Day 2 Moon Sign Gemini*

am ....

pm ....

You would be wise not to believe everything you hear today, since there are always people who have a vested interest in bending the truth. You need to be particularly careful if you are considering entering a binding commitment of any kind. At the very least you ought to read the small print.

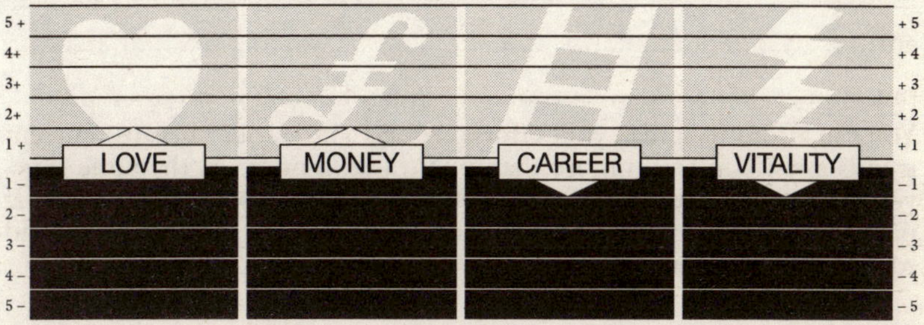

13 MONDAY *Moon Age Day 3 Moon Sign Gemini*

am ....

pm ....

It may not be easy to put your finger on potential sources of tension at the moment, though you need to ask yourself whether they have anything to do with your own restlessness. This is a time when some travel could make all the difference, though mundane events could well prevent you from making this a reality.

14 TUESDAY *Moon Age Day 4 Moon Sign Cancer*

am ....

pm ....

Now you enter a time when you should be well able to express yourself. Concern for family members is less well accented now than has been the case recently, and you can make the most of a sense of freedom. Most important of all, you have scope to implement some of those important changes to your life.

15 WEDNESDAY *Moon Age Day 5 Moon Sign Cancer*

am ....

pm ....

You have a chance to make this a significant day when it comes to busy preparations of one sort or another. Working Scorpio people should be looking for new ways to get ahead, and even contemplating new forms of responsibility. Confidence should remain generally high for most of today.

16 THURSDAY *Moon Age Day 6 Moon Sign Leo*

am ....

pm ....

You can afford to spread your efforts around a little today because current trends assist you to do more than one thing at once. At the same time, you need to register connections between specific aspects of your life. It pays to capitalise on the fact that your understanding of others is second to none at the moment.

17 FRIDAY *Moon Age Day 7 Moon Sign Leo*

am ....

pm ....

If there is one area of your life that might be described as stressful at the moment, it could well relate to finances. Rather than simply worrying about money, your best option is to undertake a sensible and deep review of your bank account. Beware of criticising friends, even if you think they are making mistakes.

18 SATURDAY *Moon Age Day 8 Moon Sign Leo*

am ....

pm ....

Now is the time to bring some of your long-term plans to fruition. You can afford to look at the broader picture of life, and needn't be so held back by immediate concerns as may have been the case recently. Be willing to listen to a rational point of view today, even if it comes from an unexpected direction.

19 SUNDAY *Moon Age Day 9 Moon Sign Virgo*

am ....

pm ....

Your love life should represent a definite high point at the moment. Make the most of this by speaking magic words in the way only someone born under Scorpio can, and then watch someone melt into your arms. Getting on with people at almost any level shouldn't turn out to be much of a problem on this Sunday.

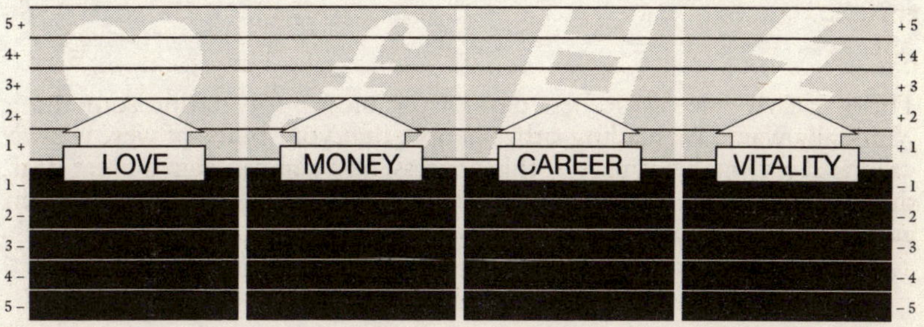

20 MONDAY *Moon Age Day 10 Moon Sign Virgo*

am..

pm..

It's natural for worries about family life to get in the way of personal freedoms from time to time, though you should still be able to make some headway today. Don't be too ready to jump to conclusions, especially where your friends are concerned. Responding immediately to gossip is not your best course of action now.

21 TUESDAY *Moon Age Day 11 Moon Sign Libra*

am..

pm..

Intimate contacts remain promising, though you needn't forget about more practical matters and have potential to make gains at work. If there seems to be a lack of excitement in your life at present, perhaps it's time to change the situation by pushing the bounds of the normal in some way.

22 WEDNESDAY *Moon Age Day 12 Moon Sign Libra*

am..

pm..

This would be a fairly appropriate time to get on with something especially interesting – in fact, it may be the only way to avoid boredom! There are good reasons to seek suggestions from family members or maybe good friends. This part of the week should be a social affair, and offers diversity for those Scorpions who are willing to look for it.

23 THURSDAY *Moon Age Day 13 Moon Sign Scorpio*

am..

pm..

This is clearly one of the best days of the month for getting something you really want. Persuading other people that your point of view is both valid and reasonable is part of this process, and you can gain a great deal, simply from being in the right place at a time when a few well-chosen words can work wonders.

24 FRIDAY *Moon Age Day 14 Moon Sign Scorpio*

am ....

pm ....

As the lunar low continues there is still luck available, so don't be afraid to take the odd chance. It's simply a question of making sure these are well considered. The sarcastic side of Scorpio should be taking a holiday this week, assisting you in your efforts to achieve an even greater level of popularity.

25 SATURDAY *Moon Age Day 15 Moon Sign Sagittarius*

am ....

pm ....

A strong thirst for new experiences is indicated. This is partly a response to the advancing year, though the main influence is the position of Mars. Today is also a chance to recognise the feelings of happiness and pride that you have towards family members, and to make efforts to repay some old debts, of various kinds.

26 SUNDAY *Moon Age Day 16 Moon Sign Sagittarius*

am ....

pm ....

Sunday is here, and if you are away from work this would be an excellent time to do some exploring. It's a question of finding places to go and some interesting people to be with. What isn't recommended at present is to fill your time with pointless tasks that don't give you the opportunity to achieve anything.

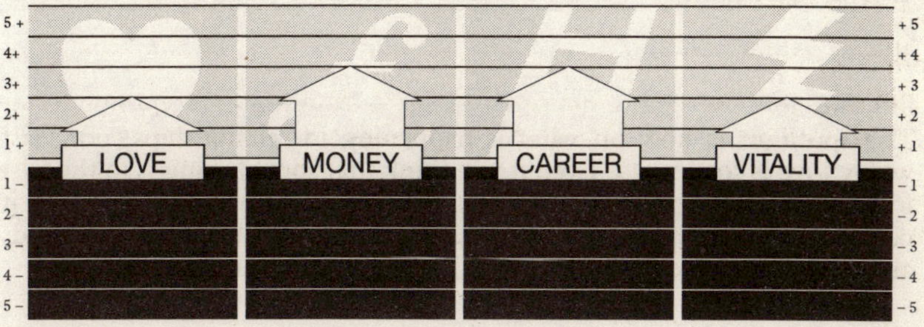

27 MONDAY *Moon Age Day 17 Moon Sign Capricorn*

am..

pm..

Certain information you obtain from colleagues, or perhaps even superiors, could prove to be very useful around now. It is definitely time to keep your eyes and ears open and to react quickly to changing circumstances. As the week gets started, your strong intuition should help you to predict the behaviour of others.

28 TUESDAY *Moon Age Day 18 Moon Sign Capricorn*

am..

pm..

Now is a time to really take stock of where you are going, and how you intend to get there. This is particularly relevant for your working life. Some Scorpio people might decide to take the opportunity this year to change their jobs altogether. If you intend to be one of them, be prepared to put in a great deal of thought first.

29 WEDNESDAY *Moon Age Day 19 Moon Sign Aquarius*

am..

pm..

Why not take a break from busy routines? The year is getting older and the summer is almost here. Many Scorpio people will be feeling the call of the wild. If the weather is good, you might simply decide to set off and go where the will takes you. If responsibilities prevent this, even a little fresh air can make all the difference.

30 THURSDAY *Moon Age Day 20 Moon Sign Aquarius*

am..

pm..

The spotlight is now on what is happening in relationships, not least where love is concerned. Even if you think that sort of thing is in the past for you, you can still make the most of romantic opportunities. When it comes to getting things done in a general sense, tried and tested methods are the order of the day.

31 FRIDAY *Moon Age Day 21 Moon Sign Aquarius*

am..

pm..

This is an ideal time for some spring cleaning, and the slightly ruthless streak that is emphasised at the moment should assist you to get rid of anything you genuinely don't need any more. There is much to be said for checking with others before you make any drastic changes at home, to avoid causing any upset.

1 SATURDAY *Moon Age Day 22 Moon Sign Pisces*

am..

pm..

You have what it takes to convince people to take an interest in your ideas and the way you express them. The fact that you have your social reform head on should assist you to help out in a community sense. This is right up your street, because Scorpio is the best sign of the zodiac for getting things done in society.

2 SUNDAY *Moon Age Day 23 Moon Sign Pisces*

am..

pm..

This is a time for revitalising elements of your personal life and for getting them going in a direction that suits you. Clear the decks for new action in a practical sense, and don't be in the least surprised if you end up doing most of the work today. It probably isn't forced upon you – you choose it!

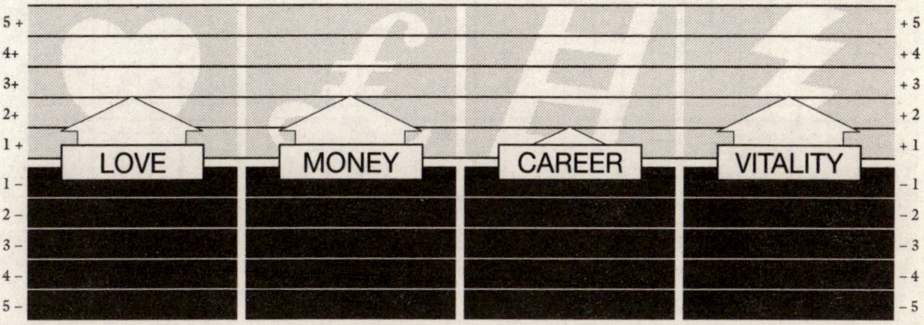

June 2013

Your Month at a Glance

(+) = Opportunities are around (−) = Be on the defensive (●) = Life is pretty ordinary

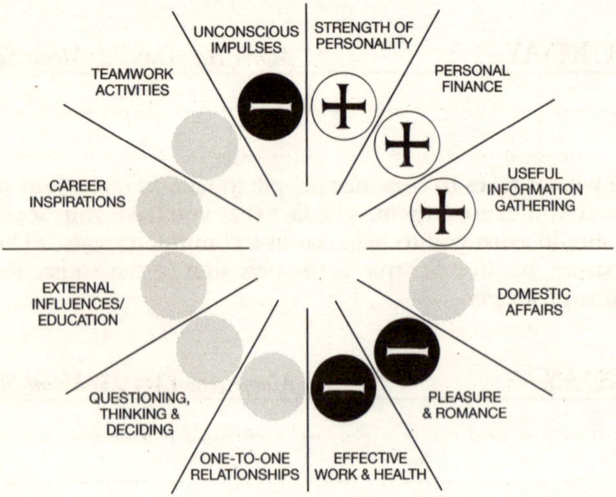

June Highs and Lows

Here I show you how the rhythms of the Moon will affect you this month. Like the tide, your energies and abilities will rise and fall with its pattern. When it is above the centre line, go for it, when it is below, you should be resting.

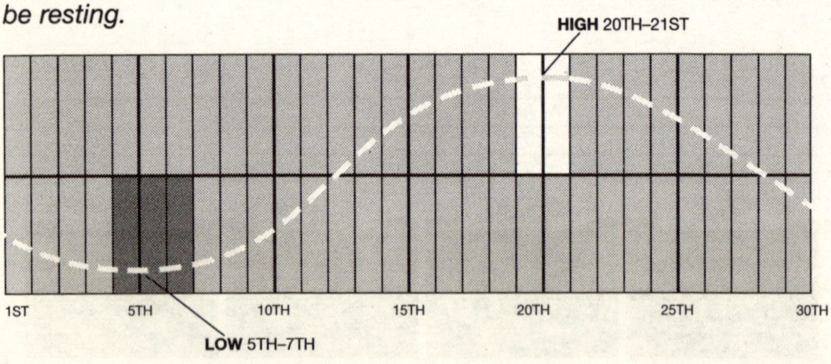

3 MONDAY *Moon Age Day 24 Moon Sign Aries*

am..

pm..

Career matters could now prove to be a test of your patience, though this needn't be the case for long. You are able to make a good impression on the world at large and can afford to go to great lengths in order to show others what you are made of. The competitive elements in your nature are clearly to the fore.

4 TUESDAY *Moon Age Day 25 Moon Sign Aries*

am..

pm..

Be prepared to overcome a few disagreements now. In fact, getting involved in arguments in the first place is probably best avoided. You would be better advised to go to almost any lengths to keep the peace. This could well mean biting your tongue, something that doesn't come easily under current influences.

5 WEDNESDAY *Moon Age Day 26 Moon Sign Taurus*

am..

pm..

Today works best if you can persuade others to take some of the major decisions. With the Moon in your opposite sign of Taurus, it might be difficult to remain in a positive frame of mind. That doesn't necessarily mean this has to be an unpleasant day, even if you do decide to take a back seat.

6 THURSDAY *Moon Age Day 27 Moon Sign Taurus*

am..

pm..

The lunar low could convince you to slow things down. If you feel there is very little you can do about a situation, perhaps it would be better not to try. Instead, settle back and take a break. That might not be very easy on a normal working day, so it's up to you to find people who are willing to take the strain for you.

7 FRIDAY *Moon Age Day 28 Moon Sign Taurus*

am ....

pm ....

With the Sun still firmly in your solar eighth house you, this would be an ideal period to make specific changes. These need to be thought out carefully, and especially so if they have a bearing on your personal life. If you are unsure of yourself, there's nothing wrong with seeking an alternative opinion.

8 SATURDAY *Moon Age Day 0 Moon Sign Gemini*

am ....

pm ....

Ups and downs in finances are a distinct possibility, and you should be ready to address these during today. In other respects you can keep life ticking along in a fairly routine way, that is, unless you decide to put in that extra bit of effort that can make all the difference. Social prospects are well accented.

9 SUNDAY *Moon Age Day 1 Moon Sign Gemini*

am ....

pm ....

Firming up financial matters is made easier with co-operation and a little extra thought on your part. Avoid doing anything that could be seen as interfering, because ending up on the wrong side of certain individuals is not helpful at this time. Why not arrange to do something very different this evening?

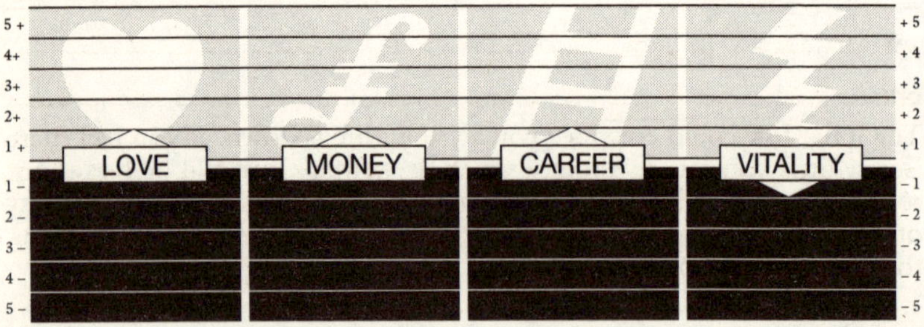

10 MONDAY *Moon Age Day 2 Moon Sign Cancer*

am..

pm..

Attending to a variety of tasks shouldn't be difficult at the beginning of this working week. You are in a position to look at life with a very practised eye and should be willing to address any problems that you encounter now. Such are your present abilities that you might be taking on the work of others as well as your own!

11 TUESDAY *Moon Age Day 3 Moon Sign Cancer*

am..

pm..

Don't be surprised if you can't complete everything on your personal agenda quite as quickly or efficiently as you wish today. It's worth sorting through necessary matters and dealing first with what is truly important. Spending at least some time with loved ones should also be on your list of priorities.

12 WEDNESDAY *Moon Age Day 4 Moon Sign Cancer*

am..

pm..

It would be best to maintain your low profile and to wait for more favourable circumstances before trying to push forward with any specific, new project. It's natural to be concerned for family members, and simply talking things through carefully can work wonders. You could discover you are worrying about nothing.

13 THURSDAY *Moon Age Day 5 Moon Sign Leo*

am..

pm..

You could do worse today than to take off to somewhere different. There are plenty of possibilities, and the more you think about them, the more options you should come up with. However, you need to avoid trying to do everything at once, a course of action that could well lead to exhaustion.

14 FRIDAY *Moon Age Day 6 Moon Sign Leo*

am ....

pm..

Career prospects are well marked, and this would be an ideal time to show superiors what you are made of. You should also be on the look-out for the chance to take on new responsibilities. Having confidence in your own abilities is what today is all about, and there are gains to be made if you ask the right questions.

15 SATURDAY *Moon Age Day 7 Moon Sign Virgo*

am ....

pm..

Idealism is all very well, but when it comes to personal matters a realistic view is sometimes required. Be ready to offer congratulations where appropriate to someone within your family or friendship circle. Trends encourage Scorpio to be in a party mood now, and socially speaking you have rarely been better.

16 SUNDAY *Moon Age Day 8 Moon Sign Virgo*

am ....

pm..

Bear in mind that parts of your inner life are now open to review. There are chinks in your armour, through which others can gain a much better understanding of what actually makes you tick. Even if this isn't the most comfortable situation as far as you are concerned, it can be very illuminating to the world at large.

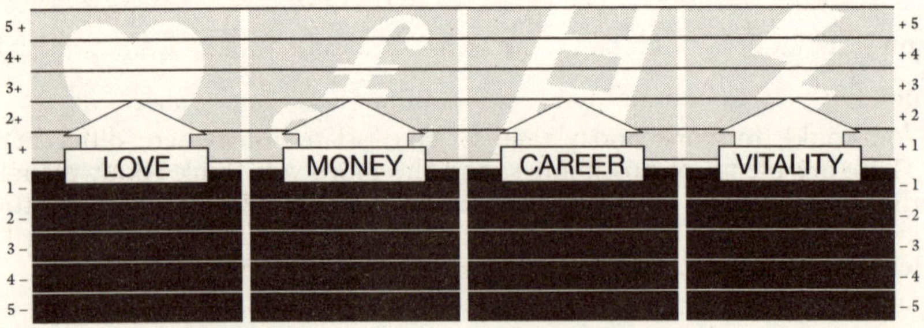

17 MONDAY *Moon Age Day 9 Moon Sign Virgo*

am..

pm..

You have scope to be the life and soul of the party now, and this assists your efforts to have a good time. The spotlight is on your growing confidence and your ability to reach destinations that would have seemed impossible once upon a time. By all means gloat a little, but recognise that there is still much to be done.

18 TUESDAY *Moon Age Day 10 Moon Sign Libra*

am..

pm..

A variety of interests now assist you to get the very most out of your life in a holistic sense. After a slightly different sort of day yesterday, the gentler side of your nature is now emphasised. Finding ways to fill your time shouldn't be at all difficult, at least not if you are willing to involve your friends in the situation.

19 WEDNESDAY *Moon Age Day 11 Moon Sign Libra*

am..

pm..

Your powers may be limited at this stage of the week, mainly because the Moon is in your solar twelfth house. This encourages a rather quieter approach than you have taken recently, but also allows a more contemplative frame of mind. Find moments to reassure your loved ones and friends that all is well.

20 THURSDAY *Moon Age Day 12 Moon Sign Scorpio*

am...

pm...

It pays to get cracking as early in the day as you can. If you know something is possible, you needn't take no for an answer, and can go that extra mile to get what you want. All of this is the gift of the lunar high, which is very potent this time around. Utilising the luck that is available doesn't necessarily mean you have to gamble.

21 FRIDAY *Moon Age Day 13 Moon Sign Scorpio*

am ....

pm..

Freedom of movement is now more crucial than ever. The Moon is presently in your zodiac sign, positively demanding that you take responsibility for your life in every sense of the word. An active and enterprising approach is the order of the day, allowing you to think up ideas at this stage that will pay dividends later.

22 SATURDAY *Moon Age Day 14 Moon Sign Sagittarius*

am ....

pm..

In a financial sense, there are signs that you could now be in the dark. If other people are running the show, it's really up to you to ask a few leading questions. On a more personal front, be prepared to respond in encounters with those you find immensely attractive. Who knows? The feeling could be mutual!

23 SUNDAY *Moon Age Day 15 Moon Sign Sagittarius*

am ....

pm..

Money-making opportunities should not be ignored this weekend. The focus is on strengthening your finances and increasing your income, and you can help your efforts by finding trustworthy allies. Any ideas you have are worth considering, so be ready to talk them over with someone you know well and rate highly.

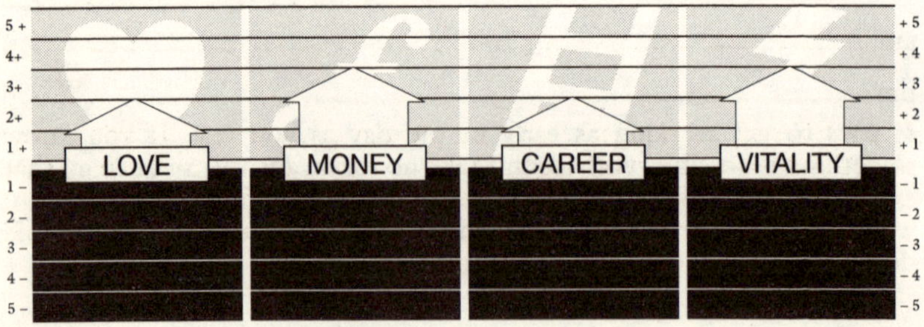

24 MONDAY *Moon Age Day 16 Moon Sign Capricorn*

am ....

pm ....

Positive influences regarding some of your deep-seated ambitions are now in play. You can take advantage of the potential for advancement at present, especially in your work. If you are a student, now is the time to apply maximum effort in order to get the results that your hard work truly deserves.

25 TUESDAY *Moon Age Day 17 Moon Sign Capricorn*

am ....

pm ....

Be prepared to deal with pressures coming from above. It is true that you have the ability to get on well in a practical sense, but that won't necessarily please everyone. Diplomacy is the key in such situations. Rather than arguing in order to get what you want, it pays to be flexible in your attitude.

26 WEDNESDAY *Moon Age Day 18 Moon Sign Aquarius*

am ....

pm ....

If you can stay on the right side of people with power, you won't do yourself any harm at all right now. This doesn't have to involve being a 'creep', but merely calls for you to show how polite you can be. Casual conversations can assist you to glean new ideas, and you also have scope to forge a new partnership of some sort.

27 THURSDAY ☿ *Moon Age Day 19 Moon Sign Aquarius*

am ....

pm ....

Even if plenty of people are on your wavelength today, you can't expect that this will be universally the case. It is important to realise that some people are never going to adopt your point of view. Stop trying to make converts and conserve your energy. Concentrate on those who are already on your side.

28 FRIDAY ☿ *Moon Age Day 20 Moon Sign Pisces*

am..

pm..

Keep your ears open for good news on the family front today. Home is where the heart is, more so for Scorpio than for just about any other zodiac sign. However, it's important to recognise that you can't carry your house around with you like a tortoise. Balancing the requirements of today won't be easy.

29 SATURDAY ☿ *Moon Age Day 21 Moon Sign Pisces*

am..

pm..

The weekend offers further possibilities in terms of travel and ideal opportunities to get some fresh air. If you are a sporting Scorpio, your competitive efforts are well accented now. No matter what your proclivities, you should stand a better chance of enjoying yourself if you can get away from routines.

30 SUNDAY ♀ *Moon Age Day 22 Moon Sign Aries*

am..

pm..

This is a time during which you can afford to pursue more personal interests and allow practicalities to take something of a back seat. Every Scorpio needs to retreat into his or her own world now and again, and this is such a period. Do what you have to do out there in the world, but then be happy to sink into your inner self.

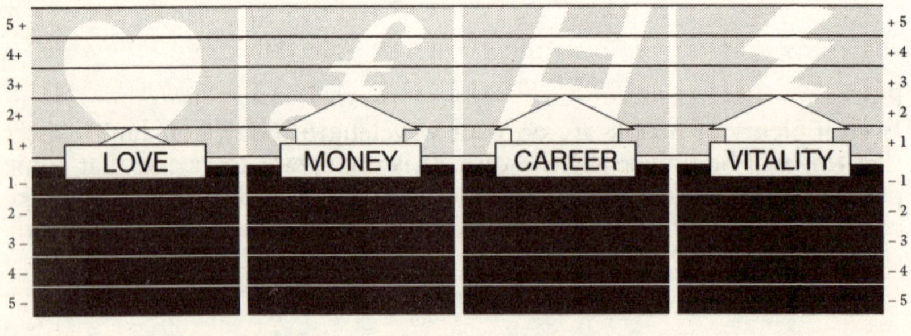

July

2013

Your Month at a Glance

(+) = Opportunities are around (−) = Be on the defensive (●) = Life is pretty ordinary

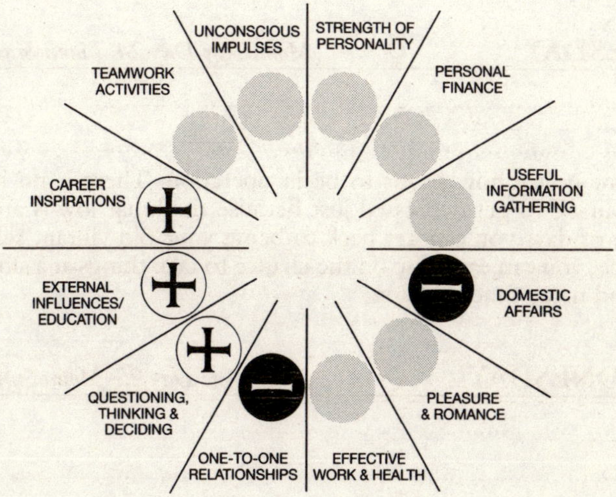

July Highs and Lows

Here I show you how the rhythms of the Moon will affect you this month. Like the tide, your energies and abilities will rise and fall with its pattern. When it is above the centre line, go for it, when it is below, you should be resting.

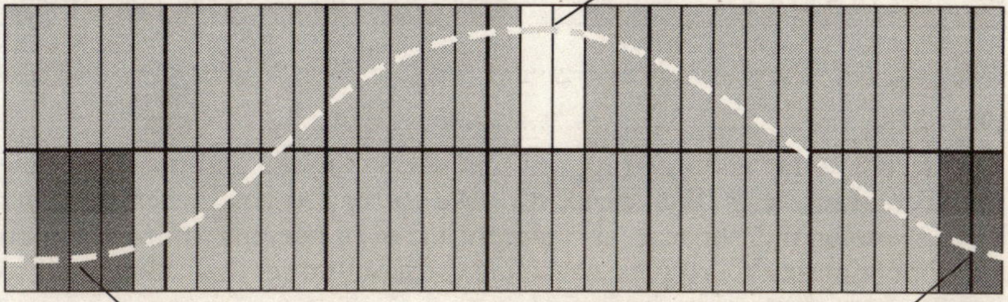

1 MONDAY ☿ *Moon Age Day 23 Moon Sign Aries*

am ....

pm ....

The spotlight is now on your willingness to get to grips with certain serious issues. However, you needn't allow such matters to get in the way of your natural enjoyment of the day in a social sense. It's a question of mixing as freely as you can at the moment and with as many different types as possible.

2 TUESDAY ☿ *Moon Age Day 24 Moon Sign Taurus*

am ....

pm ....

A go-slow policy now seems to be in operation. There is no reason to allow yourself to get depressed just because the lunar low is around. In a couple of days you can get back to being your old vibrant self. In the meantime, you can capitalise on the chance to take things at a slower pace and spend more time thinking.

3 WEDNESDAY ☿ *Moon Age Day 25 Moon Sign Taurus*

am ....

pm ....

Take one job at a time and don't expect to rush ahead at this stage of the working week. Once again, getting some rest would be no bad thing, though that might be difficult on a working day. Can you persuade others to make some of the running? This should allow you to seek out the right solution to a few problems.

4 THURSDAY ☿ *Moon Age Day 26 Moon Sign Taurus*

am ....

pm ....

The accent today is on getting out and about socially and pursuing new intellectual interests. You shouldn't have to try too hard when it comes to the new or the unusual – it's simply a case of keeping your eyes open for opportunities. Curb your natural enthusiasm rather than allowing it to get you into dangerous situations!

5 FRIDAY ☿ *Moon Age Day 27 Moon Sign Gemini*

am..

pm..

Current trends assist you to keep yourself in the picture when it comes to plans and schemes that have been crossing your mind of late. Even if not everyone is interested in what you have to say at the moment, that needn't matter. The most important thing is to discover what your dream really is, and then to go for it.

6 SATURDAY ☿ *Moon Age Day 28 Moon Sign Gemini*

am..

pm..

Today is an opportunity to create more fun on the home front than has been the case recently. It's a question of being willing to settle and less inclined to be gadding about all the time, and this should assist you to get to know loved ones even better. Romantic overtones are also highlighted in intimate relationships now.

7 SUNDAY ☿ *Moon Age Day 0 Moon Sign Cancer*

am..

pm..

The emphasis now is on leisure and pleasure. If you can't get the people you wish into a party mood, you might decide to look somewhere else instead. Trends encourage you to take a more dominant role in life this month, and today is a chance to show others that this is exactly what you are willing to do.

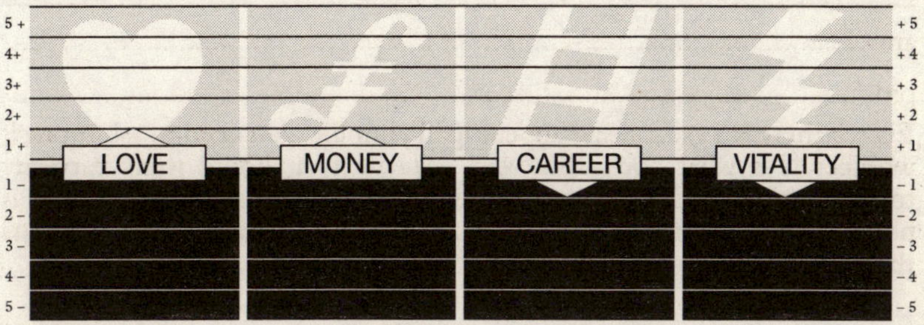

8 MONDAY ☿ *Moon Age Day 1 Moon Sign Cancer*

am ....

pm ....

It's time to consider whether it's necessary to rethink a plan of action in order to further the general progress in your life. Efficiency and organisation would help, but these might be out of the window on account of your general responsibilities towards those around you. Keep up your efforts to get out and about more.

9 TUESDAY ☿ *Moon Age Day 2 Moon Sign Cancer*

am ....

pm ....

Be prepared to deal with challenges and situations that test your ability and progressive qualities. In the main these experiences are positive, as they give you the chance to show how well you can perform, even at new tasks. A day to demonstrate your level of self-assurance and your ability to move a range of obstacles.

10 WEDNESDAY ☿ *Moon Age Day 3 Moon Sign Leo*

am ....

pm ....

You are in a position to maintain a high profile at the moment. It's time to ensure that people coming and going in your life take more notice of your presence, to be willing to give advice if you are asked. At work an active approach is best, and that might involve passing on your pearls of wisdom to important people.

11 THURSDAY ☿ *Moon Age Day 4 Moon Sign Leo*

am ....

pm ....

Even if there is a great deal happening in your life, you need to ask yourself whether it is what you really want. Maybe you should think carefully today about incentives that are either planned or already under way. It is possible that you are doing a lot but actually making few achievements that you find personally pleasing.

12 FRIDAY ☿ *Moon Age Day 5 Moon Sign Virgo*

am ....

pm ....

No matter how well you plan for today, confusion is always a possibility. It's important to be ready to deal with this, while ensuring your own actions are not contributing to the situation. You would be wise to remain patient and optimistic, and to make the most of the opportunities offered by altered circumstances.

13 SATURDAY ☿ *Moon Age Day 6 Moon Sign Virgo*

am ....

pm ....

You could do far worse this weekend than to get away from it all. While trends suggest that the company of strangers may not appeal, you can gain a great deal from more intimate relationships. There is a competitive side to your nature when it comes to sporting activities, which may seem attractive today.

14 SUNDAY ☿ *Moon Age Day 7 Moon Sign Virgo*

am ....

pm ....

Freedom is the key to happiness, which is why this would be an ideal time for Scorpio people to choose to take a holiday. If that isn't possible, why not broaden your horizons in some other way? One option is to take time out to do something that really interests you and that allows you to turn your mind away from worries.

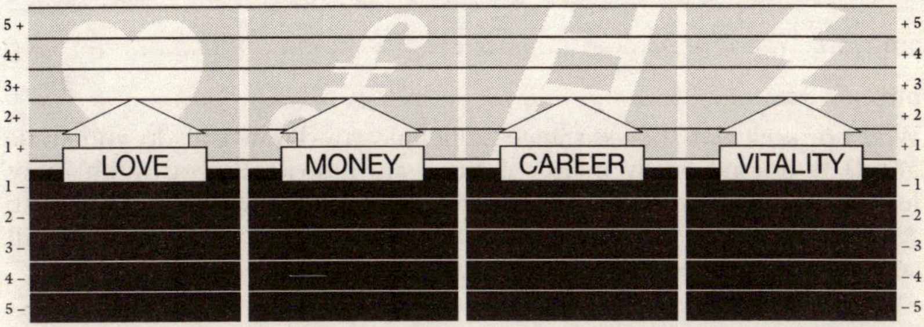

15 MONDAY ☿ *Moon Age Day 8 Moon Sign Libra*

am..

pm..

Look out for professional opportunities that offer a signpost towards future successes. Keep all options open and avoid getting bogged down too much with routines at this time. Two-way communication of all types is particularly well accented now, and can help you to learn a great deal about the way your own mind is working.

16 TUESDAY ☿ *Moon Age Day 9 Moon Sign Libra*

am..

pm..

Professionally speaking, you are able to make the best of the Sun, which is in your tenth house at the moment. It stays there until after the 20th, assisting you to get ahead in a number of different ways. There are good reasons to offer support to others, and you might even be able benefit from the arrangement yourself.

17 WEDNESDAY ☿ *Moon Age Day 10 Moon Sign Scorpio*

am..

pm..

It's time to put the finishing touches to any plans that have been up in the air for quite some time. The Moon is in your sign, and it's a marvellous opportunity to test your general luck. You can't expect to be able to deal with absolutely everyone, though you have what it takes to persuade plenty of people to follow your lead.

18 THURSDAY ☿ *Moon Age Day 11 Moon Sign Scorpio*

am..

pm..

Why not seek out the assistance of people you know can do you some good? It doesn't really matter if these are individuals you might have feared in the past, because right now you have the ability to talk to anyone. The sheer scale of your potential successes at the moment might come as a surprise – especially to you!

19 FRIDAY ☿ *Moon Age Day 12 Moon Sign Sagittarius*

am ....

pm ....

You might have to work pretty hard for anything you really want today, but you needn't let that fact worry you too much. It's a question of using all your available energy, together with the sort of determination that few can better, to make a real splash. This would be another ideal time for a Scorpio holiday.

20 SATURDAY ☿ *Moon Age Day 13 Moon Sign Sagittarius*

am ....

pm ....

A broadening of mental horizons is now available, together with a greater willingness to tell those around you how you really feel about certain matters. Coming clean can make you feel better, and it also allows you to give friends and relatives alike a better understanding of what really makes you tick.

21 SUNDAY *Moon Age Day 14 Moon Sign Capricorn*

am ....

pm ....

Your urge to enjoy personal freedoms is emphasised right now, which is not really too unusual for the zodiac sign of Scorpio. In any sort of dispute, it's important to discover who your friends really are. Don't be surprised if some of them come from quite unexpected directions under present planetary influences.

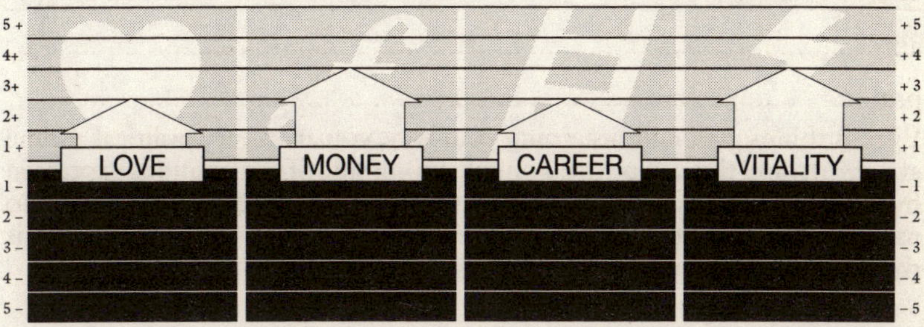

22 MONDAY *Moon Age Day 15 Moon Sign Capricorn*

am..

pm..

You have an opportunity to achieve a positive start to the working week. Be willing to put yourself out to help others, particularly people you know to be deserving of your effort and time. In a social sense, the spotlight is firmly on your sense of humour. Don't be surprised if you manage to attract some extra attention now.

23 TUESDAY *Moon Age Day 16 Moon Sign Aquarius*

am..

pm..

You may well have to deal with some genuine opposition today, perhaps with regard to plans you want to put into action. If you occupy any sort of public position, the flak is that much harder to avoid. With not enough time to do everything you want, it's necessary to be quite selective regarding your efforts.

24 WEDNESDAY *Moon Age Day 17 Moon Sign Aquarius*

am..

pm..

Does something seem to be missing from your life today? Perhaps it is the company of certain family members, or friends who are far away. You might have to rely much more on your own opinions, though the experience does you a great deal of good in the longer term and can help to strengthen your convictions.

25 THURSDAY *Moon Age Day 18 Moon Sign Pisces*

am..

pm..

Even if things generally are going your way, you are a very political animal at present, and this can put you on the wrong side of the opinions expressed by others. It can sometimes feel as though you are being criticised, no matter what you decide to do. Take no notice – the important thing is that you pitch in and try.

26 FRIDAY *Moon Age Day 19 Moon Sign Pisces*

am...

pm...

By all means take advantage of a busy social scene, though that might make it rather difficult for you to manage everything you want to do. Allowing certain activities to take a back seat would be no bad thing. Since this is the summer, you might simply decide that indoor pursuits are better suited to the colder months.

27 SATURDAY *Moon Age Day 20 Moon Sign Aries*

am...

pm...

This is another potentially busy period and a time when it is entirely possible that you will be trying to achieve more than is good for you. Go slowly, and take the advice of those who suggest you need a rest. Even after an hour or two, you should be feeling better and can make full use of your second wind.

28 SUNDAY *Moon Age Day 21 Moon Sign Aries*

am...

pm...

There are influences around at the moment that encourage you to show the home-loving side of your Scorpio nature. Although it's tempting to try to do a host of different things, in your heart you probably want to be with those you love the most. There is much to be gained by taking a well-earned break.

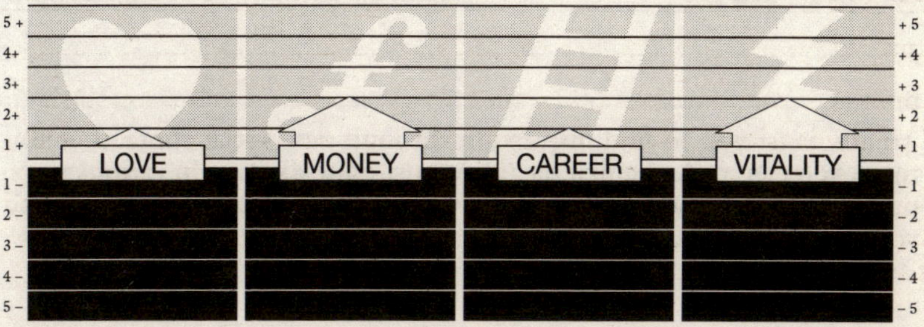

29 MONDAY *Moon Age Day 22 Moon Sign Aries*

am ....

pm ....

Independent efforts in the social sphere can now enable you to break away from a reliance on certain other people. Be prepared to respond to some leading questions about your actions. It may simply be that you don't trust someone quite as much as you once did, and you are right to look after your own interests.

30 TUESDAY *Moon Age Day 23 Moon Sign Taurus*

am ....

pm ....

There are limitations to contend with, though they needn't hold you back too much. It's important to keep busy today, but not to bite off more than you can chew. Social trends remain positive, and you are encouraged to create good times in the company of people who have always had the ability to make you laugh.

31 WEDNESDAY *Moon Age Day 24 Moon Sign Taurus*

am ....

pm ....

Despite the continuing lunar low, joint financial matters of all sorts are extremely well highlighted. In addition, you can get through far more work than you could possibly have expected. You have the ability to find plenty of shortcuts now, and it's also worth enlisting the help and support of some very useful types.

1 THURSDAY *Moon Age Day 25 Moon Sign Gemini*

am ....

pm ....

Trends assist you to find inspiration through new social contacts at this time. You can make the first day of August quite exciting in various ways, particularly with the weekend in view. Now the summer is truly here and you need to be ready for the restless side of your nature to start to show.

2 FRIDAY *Moon Age Day 26 Moon Sign Gemini*

am ....

pm ....

A sense of impatience is a natural reaction today, particularly if you have allowed yourself to be tied down by too many obligations. What could really appeal is the freedom to do whatever you wish, as much as possible. You have everything you need to become the life and soul of the party now.

3 SATURDAY *Moon Age Day 27 Moon Sign Gemini*

am ....

pm ....

You can definitely increase your chances of getting ahead by being in the right company. The more you give out to the world at large, the greater are the benefits that come back to you. Beware of getting tied down with pointless details, and use this Saturday to please others, as well as achieving happiness yourself on the way.

4 SUNDAY *Moon Age Day 28 Moon Sign Cancer*

am ....

pm ....

Make the most of career opportunities now and get ahead of tasks before they become due. With plenty of energy available, and a real determination to fill every available minute with activity, you needn't let much hold you back. What you do have to remember is that it is quite possible to run yourself ragged! Balance in everything is crucial.

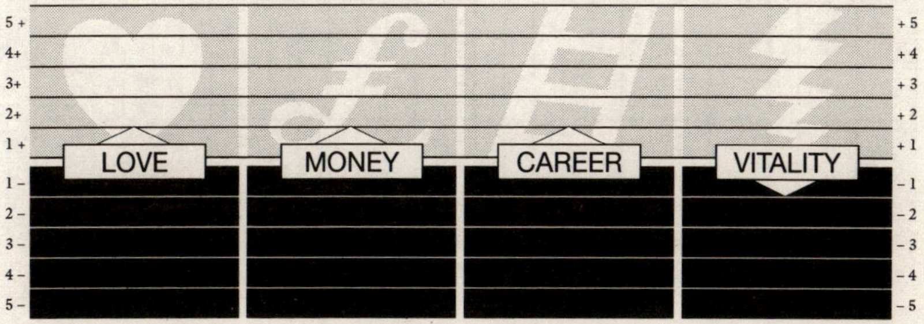

August

2013

Your Month at a Glance

(+) = Opportunities are around (–) = Be on the defensive (●) = Life is pretty ordinary

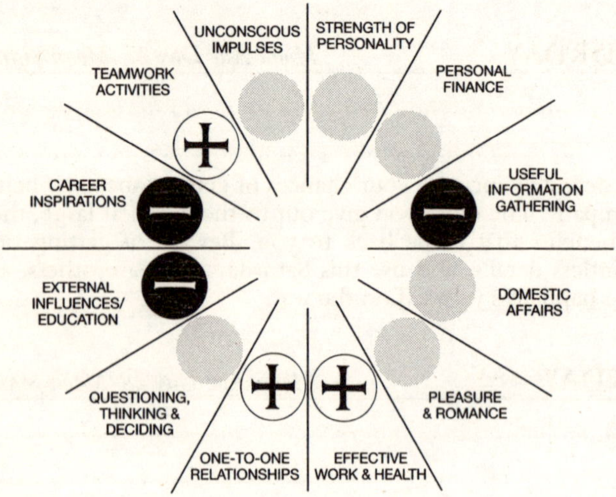

August Highs and Lows

Here I show you how the rhythms of the Moon will affect you this month. Like the tide, your energies and abilities will rise and fall with its pattern. When it is above the centre line, go for it, when it is below, you should be resting.

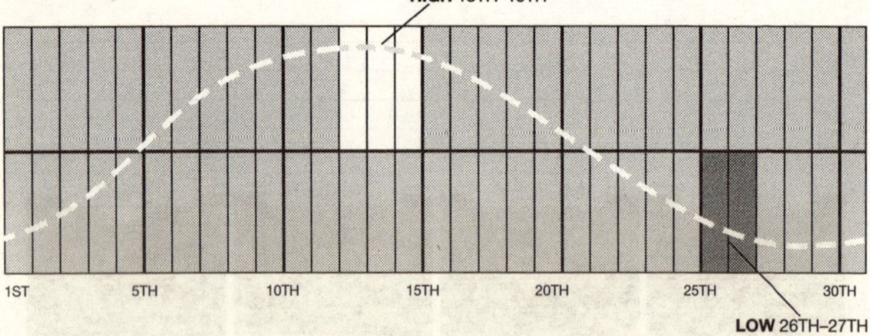

5 MONDAY *Moon Age Day 29 Moon Sign Cancer*

am ....

pm ....

In the career stakes, getting ahead today should continue to be a piece of cake. Your ability to forge good relations with others is notable. It's a question of showing that you have a bright and breezy attitude to life in general and aren't taking yourself as seriously as can sometimes be the case. This should be Scorpio at its best.

6 TUESDAY *Moon Age Day 0 Moon Sign Leo*

am ....

pm ....

There's nothing wrong with looking again at a recent project. You might even decide it would be better all round to start again from scratch. Far from being a chore, you need to ensure that you view this as a labour of love. Do a little of this and a bit of that today, in order to keep life balanced.

7 WEDNESDAY *Moon Age Day 1 Moon Sign Leo*

am ....

pm ....

If you make the most of the good luck that is available, it might seem as though you can't put a foot wrong. Actually you can, and need to bear this fact in mind before you push too hard. At the same time there is no need to withdraw into deeply cautious mode. Once again, balance is the key, but you will need to concentrate.

8 THURSDAY *Moon Age Day 2 Moon Sign Leo*

am ....

pm ....

You should have little difficulty identifying exactly what interests you at the moment. Once you have done so you can afford to march forward confidently towards a more certain future. Even if you may have quite a lot on your plate in terms of work, in a general sense you should be happy to take on new tasks too.

9 FRIDAY *Moon Age Day 3 Moon Sign Virgo*

am ....

pm ....

Having worked steadily towards some of your recent objectives, you should now be in a position to reap the benefits. It's important to have the weekend in view and to find opportunities to socialise as soon as work is out of the way. It's natural to feel tired, but the important thing is to make sure you perk up again.

10 SATURDAY *Moon Age Day 4 Moon Sign Virgo*

am ....

pm ....

Your fortunes as far as friendship is concerned seem to be on the up. This is an ideal time to bring new people into your life, possibly as acquaintances first of all, but later as friends. This proves to be important, given the Scorpio knack of keeping its pals for many years. Good times are within your grasp.

11 SUNDAY *Moon Age Day 5 Moon Sign Libra*

am ....

pm ....

Being the team leader is all very well, though you need to be prepared to respond to any opposition you face. Remain in fighting form, and don't back down just because of a little criticism. However, there's nothing wrong with conceding the odd point if you know you are wrong – keep an objective frame of mind.

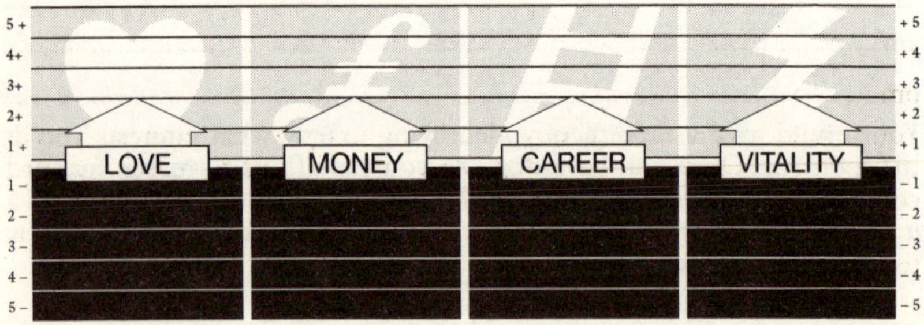

12 MONDAY *Moon Age Day 6 Moon Sign Libra*

am ....

pm ....

A day to make the best of all types of social encounters. You might even decide to bring some romantic interest into your life if you are a young or single Scorpio. Family pleasures are possible, but mixing with friends could well offer you even more today. Your sense of humour can make all the difference now.

13 TUESDAY *Moon Age Day 7 Moon Sign Scorpio*

am ....

pm ....

There are some very lucky influences on offer at the moment. The Moon is back in your sign, enhancing the energy you have available, and helping you to come up with ideas on how to use it. At both work and home you need to be on good form, willing to make a favourable impression and keen to get on with life.

14 WEDNESDAY *Moon Age Day 8 Moon Sign Scorpio*

am ....

pm ....

Socially speaking you should be on the up and up today. This part of the working week is ideal for seeking good company and for pursing some of the inspiring prospects that are on offer now. Once again travel is well starred, and being tied to the same spot for more than a few hours is not to be recommended.

15 THURSDAY *Moon Age Day 9 Moon Sign Scorpio*

am ....

pm ....

Your physical strength is noteworthy, as is your endurance. Trends highlight an urge to be in different places and a burning desire to see ever new horizons, both practically and mentally. Romance is entirely possible, even if it is the very last thing you have been looking for or expecting at this time.

16 FRIDAY *Moon Age Day 10 Moon Sign Sagittarius*

am...

pm...

There's no harm thinking a great deal about yourself today. However, it's worth making sure that you don't appear selfish when viewed from the perspective of those around you. It's almost impossible for you not to bear others in mind, though you need to make them aware of that fact too.

17 SATURDAY *Moon Age Day 11 Moon Sign Sagittarius*

am...

pm...

Your ego can be well and truly boosted today, particularly if you are attracting praise from others. Even if there are ongoing jobs that have to be done, it pays to make time to take a refreshingly new look at life. As a result, you need to be willing to rearrange your schedule if this proves to be necessary.

18 SUNDAY *Moon Age Day 12 Moon Sign Capricorn*

am...

pm...

You need to put back some of the spice of life that might seem to be missing. You can do this on a romantic or a general social level, though it may be more difficult at work. Splitting your time successfully could also be a challenge. There's a risk that situations could become intermingled and confused.

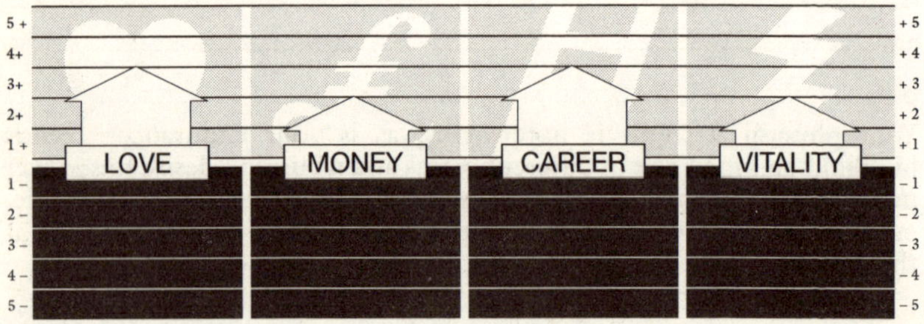

19 MONDAY *Moon Age Day 13 Moon Sign Capricorn*

am ....

pm ....

Be on the look-out for those who come new to your life at this time. This could be at work, or later when you are socialising. These people can bring a sort of message with them, which you will be wise to take on board. In reality, advice on your own life and circumstances is all around you at this time.

20 TUESDAY *Moon Age Day 14 Moon Sign Aquarius*

am ....

pm ....

Make the most of a favourable time on the professional front during which you can feel in charge and make beneficial changes. In some ways it shouldn't matter if you don't always know exactly what you are doing. The main thing is your capacity for hard work, and your willingness to use it.

21 WEDNESDAY *Moon Age Day 15 Moon Sign Aquarius*

am ....

pm ....

The Sun is now in your solar eleventh house, bringing a new period during which you can do much to enhance your social and personal life. There are good reasons to take more notice of the people who figure in your life. As well as this being potentially beneficial to you, it will probably please them too!

22 THURSDAY *Moon Age Day 16 Moon Sign Pisces*

am ....

pm ....

Slowly but surely, your life should be moving forwards, beginning to achieve a pace and a vitality that may have been somewhat lacking so far this month. By all means pace yourself, but not too much! Discussions also require a delicate balance, this time between putting forward your own opinion and yet remaining fair.

23 FRIDAY *Moon Age Day 17 Moon Sign Pisces*

am ....

pm ....

This continues to be a favourable period in most respects, though less so if you take life too seriously. It has to be said that Scorpio is not the natural comic of the zodiac, but can sometimes display a rather black sense of humour. By all means show this today, but don't expect to be everyone's cup of tea.

24 SATURDAY *Moon Age Day 18 Moon Sign Aries*

am ....

pm ....

There are good things on offer today, and you really need to make sure you are part of them. Your state of mind from the very start of the day has a role to play in this. It would be sensible to take a very optimistic view, because the image you project at the moment has a great bearing on what you are able to gain from life.

25 SUNDAY *Moon Age Day 19 Moon Sign Aries*

am ....

pm ....

You have what it takes to get communication and travel issues going your way. The auspices are particularly positive for any Scorpio people who are on holiday at this time, or else planning to go away very soon. Financial matters would benefit from some careful thought and a bit of prior planning.

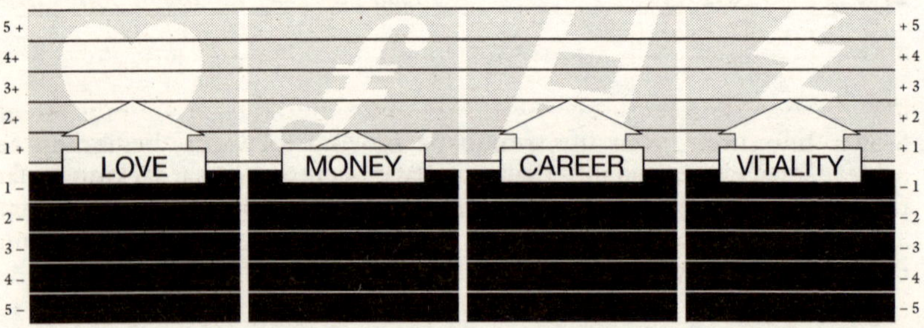

26 MONDAY *Moon Age Day 20 Moon Sign Taurus*

am ....

pm ....

Keep things simple today and don't try too hard. The lunar low this time around needn't prevent you from enjoying life to the full, but if you try to complicate matters there's a risk that you'll come unstuck. Attitude is all important, particularly if you are dealing with especially sensitive people.

27 TUESDAY *Moon Age Day 21 Moon Sign Taurus*

am ....

pm ....

Whether at work or at home, you can't expect to take everything you hear as being one hundred percent true today. A healthy scepticism is a good thing, just as long as you don't carry it too far. Even if you feel you are walking through treacle, you still have scope to make gentle progress throughout the lunar low.

28 WEDNESDAY *Moon Age Day 22 Moon Sign Gemini*

am ....

pm ....

This is a period when you can capitalise on the chance to do something unusual or different. If you are somewhat uncomfortable, perhaps because of an old war wound, it would be best to keep busy at this time. Putting things to the back of your mind appears to have become an art form for Scorpio around now.

29 THURSDAY *Moon Age Day 23 Moon Sign Gemini*

am ....

pm ....

There are influences about that assist you to get in touch with the wider social world now. Confirmation of something you suspected could well be available later in the day, though you will need to concentrate in order to realise the fact. You can afford to be busy, generally happy and quite keen to make some sort of splash.

30 FRIDAY *Moon Age Day 24 Moon Sign Gemini*

am...

pm...

Matters relating to groups come under scrutiny today. You don't always work at your best in a committee-type situation, since your co-planetary ruler is Mars, which encourages independence. However, present trends assist you to co-operate more fully at present and to contribute well in a range of situations.

31 SATURDAY *Moon Age Day 25 Moon Sign Cancer*

am...

pm...

Your desire for intimacy around now should be catered for on a romantic level, but you also have a chance to forge a new sort of closeness when in the company of friends. Even if it appears that those you meet are opening up more, perhaps it is your own attitude that has changed. Only you know the truth!

1 SUNDAY *Moon Age Day 26 Moon Sign Cancer*

am...

pm...

September arrives and brings with it a great deal of hard work for many sons and daughters of Scorpio. What's new about that? Well, it's a question of you deliberately choosing to put in the effort, partly because you know it will get you ahead of the herd. Routines can be tiresome, but they are necessary too.

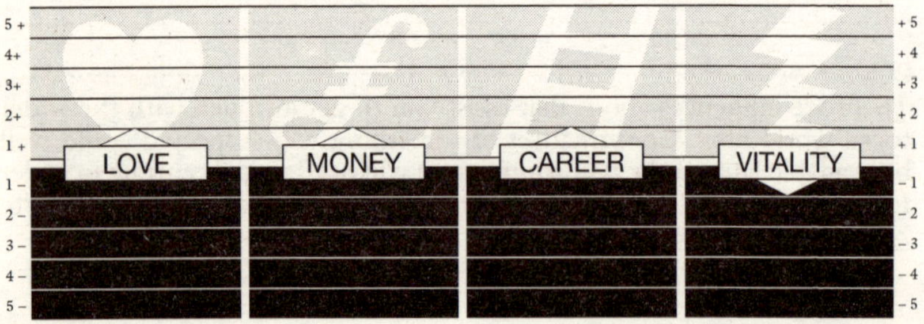

September

2013

Your Month at a Glance

(+) = Opportunities are around (–) = Be on the defensive (●) = Life is pretty ordinary

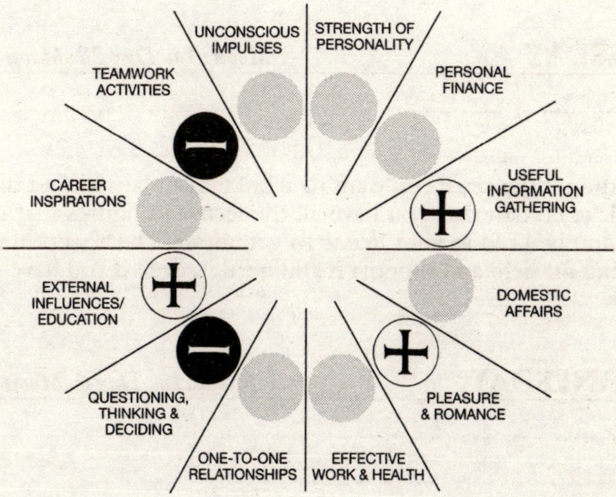

September Highs and Lows

Here I show you how the rhythms of the Moon will affect you this month. Like the tide, your energies and abilities will rise and fall with its pattern. When it is above the centre line, go for it, when it is below, you should be resting.

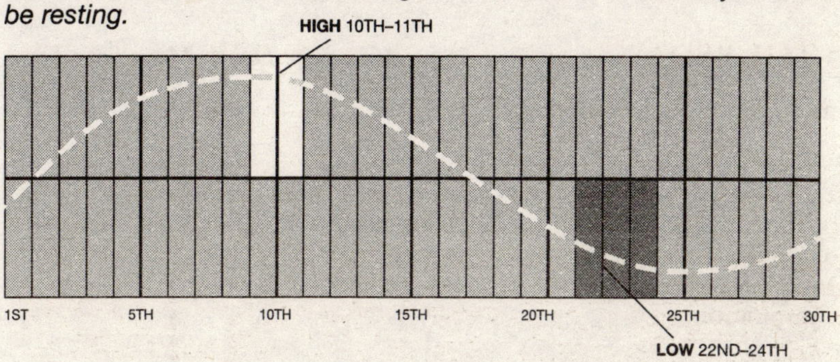

2 MONDAY *Moon Age Day 27 Moon Sign Leo*

am...

pm...

Stand by for a period during which you have a chance to interact with all manner of different types. Although, socially, you tend to be best with people you know, the more adventurous side of your zodiac sign is now to the fore. Set to doing things bright and early this morning and keep up your efforts.

3 TUESDAY *Moon Age Day 28 Moon Sign Leo*

am...

pm...

Organisation is the key if you want to avoid major plans hitting the buffers today. Make certain that you have all the facts and figures that you need to hand and be bold in your desire to get ahead. There's nothing wrong with asking for help and support if you need it, even if you have to search to find it.

4 WEDNESDAY *Moon Age Day 0 Moon Sign Leo*

am...

pm...

The impetuous side of your nature is highlighted at this stage of the week. There's nothing at all wrong with this, just as long as you don't go off the deep end. Keep your enthusiasm under some sort of wraps, and be careful not to offer offence without realising. Creative potential is especially well accented now.

5 THURSDAY *Moon Age Day 1 Moon Sign Virgo*

am...

pm...

You now have what it takes to pursue much more harmonious social and romantic encounters. Today is about using your fine sense of balance to avoid giving offence and increasing your popularity among friends. Don't be surprised if some of them are looking to you for a special sort of inspiration.

6 FRIDAY *Moon Age Day 2 Moon Sign Virgo*

am ....

pm ....

There is such a strong planetary influence on the social scene right now that you really need to make the most of it. This gives you a chance to chat away, ten to the dozen, and show how just how talkative you can really be. Most aspects of life prove to be steady, leaving time to simply have fun.

7 SATURDAY *Moon Age Day 3 Moon Sign Libra*

am ....

pm ....

You may have to pay serious attention now to financial matters. This is an area of life that may not hold much fascination for you at present. Short of winning the lottery, however, it is something you need to address. Talking things through with loved ones can help you to come up with ingenious ways to improve cash-flow.

8 SUNDAY *Moon Age Day 4 Moon Sign Libra*

am ....

pm ....

The Moon enters your twelfth house, offering a quieter spell, which could be quite welcome ahead of the lunar high in a day or two. There are moments to reassess decisions you have recently made. Intuition remains generally strong and can be your best guide, especially in terms of relationships.

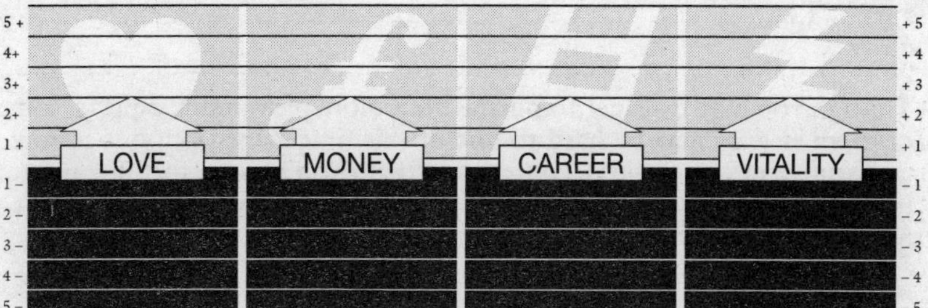

9 MONDAY *Moon Age Day 5 Moon Sign Libra*

am ....

pm ....

This could well be a fairly sluggish day and one that may not offer you a great deal of what you are looking for in life at this time. Never mind. You can afford to ask other people to help you out if necessary, and should still be able to enjoy what life has to offer on a social and personal footing.

10 TUESDAY *Moon Age Day 6 Moon Sign Scorpio*

am ....

pm ....

One of the most productive and happy periods of the year has arrived. If you aren't able to make good progress now, you need to ask yourself whether you are trying as hard as you could. There is more than a little luck available now, and what matters most about today is mixing with people you really like.

11 WEDNESDAY *Moon Age Day 7 Moon Sign Scorpio*

am ....

pm ....

As the lunar high continues, you can take advantage of another potentially promising day. If you have the chance, why not get out and about? Socially speaking you should be on top form and willing to mix with a whole range of individuals. This is definitely a time for making changes in your life, some of which could be far-reaching.

12 THURSDAY *Moon Age Day 8 Moon Sign Sagittarius*

am ....

pm ....

Though you may be eager to pursue life's more pleasurable aspects, some of them at least may be hard to find at this time. One option is to force the issue, and you could need to put in that extra bit of effort if you want to make things happen. This might well be a fairly favourable day from a financial point of view.

13 FRIDAY *Moon Age Day 9 Moon Sign Sagittarius*

am ....

pm..

Socially you need to make sure there is plenty happening. The upcoming weekend offers real alternatives, and the chance to shine in company. Putting the routines of life on the back burner would be no bad thing now. If romance calls, you need to be ready to answer. Stand by for some very special extra attention.

14 SATURDAY *Moon Age Day 10 Moon Sign Capricorn*

am ....

pm..

In terms of the competitive side of life it might be difficult to see what progress you are making under present influences. You have the ability to change this, especially if you adopt a different way of looking at old problems. It's time to use your current vitality to get a great deal done in a practical sense.

15 SUNDAY *Moon Age Day 11 Moon Sign Capricorn*

am ....

pm..

With the potential for a slight lack of confidence today, together with indications of a fairly absent-minded phase, it would be natural to feel as though you are taking two steps forward and three back. It shouldn't be long before you can get yourself fully into the swing of things. In the meantime, rely on your intuition.

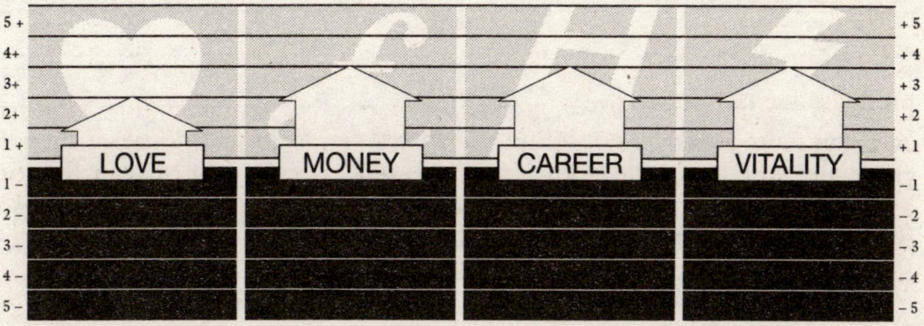

16 MONDAY *Moon Age Day 12 Moon Sign Aquarius*

am ....

pm ....

Professionally speaking you need to make the most of what can be a more progressive phase. Certain that your ambitions now seem more reasonable, you should be able to find the help you have been looking for in a specific direction. If you are out shopping today, you should keep your eyes open for a bargain.

17 TUESDAY *Moon Age Day 13 Moon Sign Aquarius*

am ....

pm ....

Trusting other people is all very well, though you do run the risk of ending up in some sort of undesirable situation. Relying on yourself is probably best for the moment, and also being prepared to make important decisions without help and advice from others. Is your concern for specific family members justified?

18 WEDNESDAY *Moon Age Day 14 Moon Sign Pisces*

am ....

pm ....

It's worth trying a variety of tasks and interests today, if only to show how flexible and capable you are. Success definitely comes through diversity as far as you are concerned, and you can also gain at the moment by simply keeping your eyes and ears open. Personally speaking, you might find you have a secret admirer.

19 THURSDAY *Moon Age Day 15 Moon Sign Pisces*

am ....

pm ....

You can gain today by confiding your personal feelings in others. This is especially true in the case of friends who have been a part of your life for a long time now. These are the sort of people you can trust and in whose judgement you have confidence. This works well as a stay-at-home day for at least some Scorpions.

20 FRIDAY *Moon Age Day 16 Moon Sign Aries*

am...

pm...

Be prepared to deal with the tiresome aspects of the day, particularly in terms of friendship. Maybe people are asking too much of you or putting you in a difficult position. Although planetary trends assist you to keep your cool, you may simply feel you have no choice but to show how you feel about the situation.

21 SATURDAY *Moon Age Day 17 Moon Sign Aries*

am...

pm...

With plenty of variety now on offer, there is no reason at all for you to be bored today. You do need to concentrate on a few important issues and should be willing to tackle any particularly thorny problems that arise in relation to your partner. Money matters may also require some inventive thought.

22 SUNDAY *Moon Age Day 18 Moon Sign Taurus*

am...

pm...

The influence of the lunar low is apt to test your patience, and puts the emphasis on the grumpier side of your nature. Most people will forgive you for that, particularly if you can also demonstrate your sense of humour through your dealings with others. This is a day of opposing possibilities.

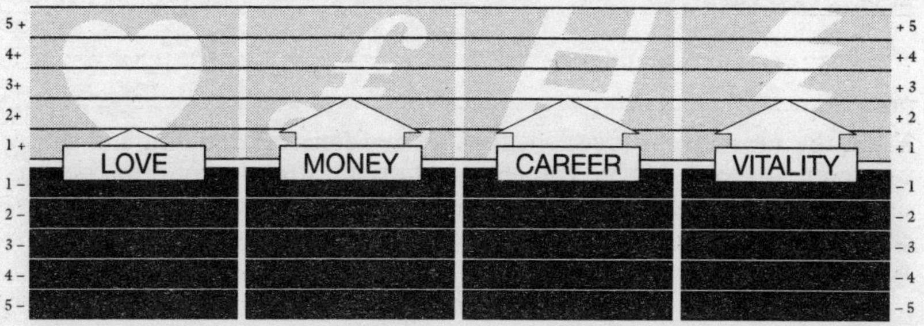

23 MONDAY *Moon Age Day 19 Moon Sign Taurus*

am ....

pm ....

This may not be the very best period of the month, especially for making progress or getting on with specific tasks. The lunar low does little to help your energy levels, though you needn't allow it to have a bearing on your social impulses. Stay around people you know and remain absolutely determined to have some fun.

24 TUESDAY *Moon Age Day 20 Moon Sign Taurus*

am ....

pm ....

Despite the fading effects of the lunar low, you do now have more scope to get what you want. Whereas you sometimes have to bully your way towards directions that seem right, at the moment you can use your silver tongue to talk people round with very few problems. Make the most of your magnetic personality!

25 WEDNESDAY *Moon Age Day 21 Moon Sign Gemini*

am ....

pm ....

Plenty of positive highlights surround social possibilities today, though making progress at work might be a different matter. It's important to identify whether this is down to your own approach, or the attitude of others. Your consideration for people who are in any form of distress is highlighted at present.

26 THURSDAY *Moon Age Day 22 Moon Sign Gemini*

am ....

pm ....

Make the most of the freedom that today offers by thinking and doing whatever you wish. Maybe you are avoiding the attention of other people, or simply taking matters into your own hands. Since creative potential is emphasised, and Venus figures in this, turning your hand to art would be no bad thing.

27 FRIDAY *Moon Age Day 23 Moon Sign Cancer*

am ....

pm ....

Even if you can sense that your domestic partner has your best interests at heart, that doesn't mean you will agree with all their suggestions. Trying to do your own thing, whilst at the same time remaining kind and tactful, may not be easy right now. The best way round the situation is to try to explain your decisions.

28 SATURDAY *Moon Age Day 24 Moon Sign Cancer*

am ....

pm ....

There is no need to be kept down today, as you can tap into a good deal more resilience than may have been the case yesterday. Nevertheless, routines probably won't appeal, nor will any task that goes against the grain. Conforming to expectations certainly isn't going to be your strong point for the next week or so.

29 SUNDAY *Moon Age Day 25 Moon Sign Cancer*

am ....

pm ....

A slightly tense atmosphere could prevail if you spend too much time trying to deal with emotional issues. The less you concentrate on specifics today, the more you can achieve. You can afford to let your confidence increase gradually, and if you're working on a Sunday you can put this to good effect.

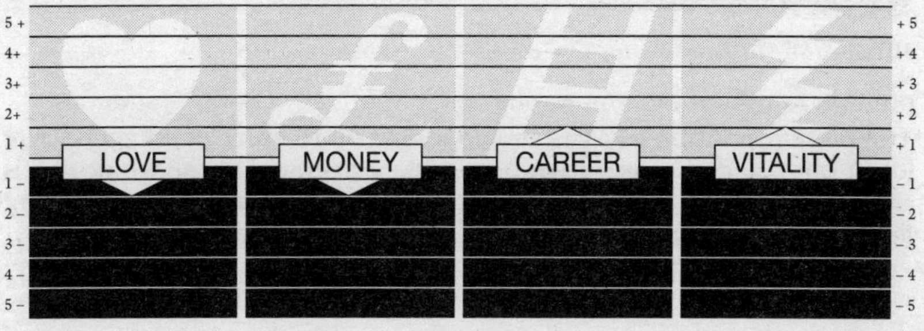

30 MONDAY *Moon Age Day 26 Moon Sign Leo*

am ....

pm ....

Trends assist you to find joy in friendship as the new working week gets started. A slight element of hesitancy is indicated, particularly when it comes to making decisions you know to be of supreme importance. However, you needn't stick fast over personal or family issues. It pays to listen to sound advice.

1 TUESDAY *Moon Age Day 27 Moon Sign Leo*

am ....

pm ....

On a personal level, you need to be ready to deal with any difficulties that arise at work. It's a question of how well you have explained your motives, and whether or not others have understood them. You can resolve this situation, but it could take some thinking about. You can afford to take a rest if you get really jaded.

2 WEDNESDAY *Moon Age Day 28 Moon Sign Virgo*

am ....

pm ....

Today you should feel freer to express yourself – in some cases perhaps too much so! Don't forget you are dealing with the feelings and emotions of those you care for the most. Being outspoken is all well and good, but you shouldn't lose sight of your sense of responsibility. Stand by to start forging some new relationships.

3 THURSDAY *Moon Age Day 29 Moon Sign Virgo*

am ....

pm ....

The present position of Mars should assist you to exert an influence over loved ones, and also over friends to a lesser degree. On the whole this is an ideal period for mixing freely with the world at large, though opting for a change of scene later in the day would be no bad thing.

4 FRIDAY *Moon Age Day 0 Moon Sign Virgo*

am...

pm...

Trends suggest it may be difficult for you to summon up much enthusiasm today. Being the person that everyone else is relying on is all very well, though it may not be a state of affairs you presently relish. Actually it's all a matter of perspective. In more cheerful times you would probably enjoy the attention!

5 SATURDAY *Moon Age Day 1 Moon Sign Libra*

am...

pm...

It's natural to question whether your assessment of personal situations is flawed in some way. However, the best time for thinking deeply about the more intimate aspects of your life would be later. For now, you are encouraged to show life a casual bat and to enjoy as much time with friends as you can manage.

6 SUNDAY *Moon Age Day 2 Moon Sign Libra*

am...

pm...

Progress in a general sense could be more difficult to achieve than you might wish, but this is only temporary until the Moon reaches your own zodiac sign tomorrow. In the meantime, you have the opportunity to think deeply about specific issues and to show a positive response to the needs of your family.

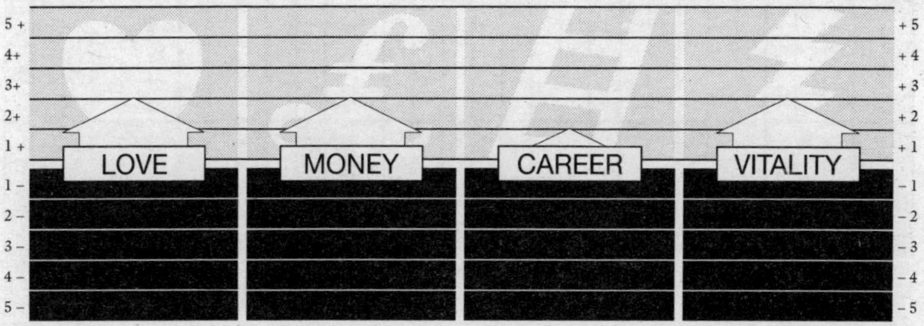

October

2013

Your Month at a Glance

⊕ = Opportunities are around   ⊖ = Be on the defensive   ● = Life is pretty ordinary

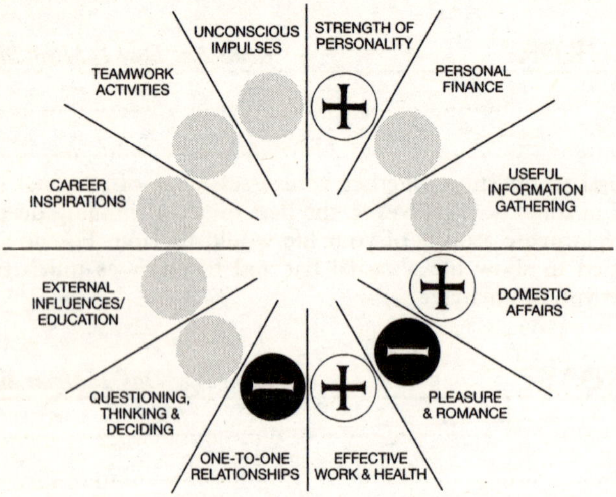

October Highs and Lows

Here I show you how the rhythms of the Moon will affect you this month. Like the tide, your energies and abilities will rise and fall with its pattern. When it is above the centre line, go for it, when it is below, you should be resting.

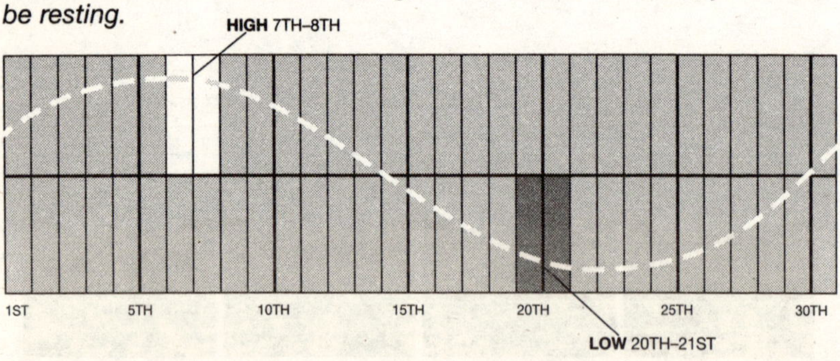

7 MONDAY *Moon Age Day 3 Moon Sign Scorpio*

am..

pm..

Make sure you make this is a Monday to remember. With plenty of good luck on offer, and the sort of confidence you sometimes only dream about, you can afford to take a few chances. With a little practical help you should be in a position to achieve a number of objectives that were closed to you before.

8 TUESDAY *Moon Age Day 4 Moon Sign Scorpio*

am..

pm..

Not simply the Moon, but especially the present position of Venus, can help to boost your confidence. The lunar high encourages you to believe in yourself much more than has been possible of late. Even if you don't make much professional progress now, in a personal sense you need to ensure you are firing on all cylinders.

9 WEDNESDAY *Moon Age Day 5 Moon Sign Sagittarius*

am..

pm..

Along comes an ideal period for exploring different possibilities, plus the chance to make progress in financial matters. The more change you can bring into your life at this time, the sooner you can take full advantage of what life has to offer. Why not throw around a few compliments and see what happens?

10 THURSDAY *Moon Age Day 6 Moon Sign Sagittarius*

am..

pm..

The spotlight is now on the way you respond to the influence of specific people in your life. The more sympathetic side of your nature is to the fore, and you may be more willing to help people you didn't feel too sorry for previously. A little discrimination would be no bad thing when you are picking new allies.

11 FRIDAY *Moon Age Day 7 Moon Sign Capricorn*

am ....

pm..

In terms of self-expression, an ebullient attitude is all very well at the moment, though it pays to exercise a little self-control if you don't want that Scorpio nature to get you into trouble. You can't expect everyone to be especially helpful, and you need to be prepared to work hard on your own behalf now.

12 SATURDAY *Moon Age Day 8 Moon Sign Capricorn*

am ....

pm..

The best way to ensure that others don't get hold of the wrong end of the stick at present is simply to explain yourself carefully. Whatever attitude you decide to adopt, it's always worth bearing in mind how others will perceive you. A day to settle down and spend some time with people you like and trust.

13 SUNDAY *Moon Age Day 9 Moon Sign Aquarius*

am ....

pm..

Times are changing, and now your personal power and effectiveness are well accented. After a few days during which progress might have been difficult, you now have scope to push forward more successfully. This can be applied in all areas of your life, but can be especially relevant for personal attachments.

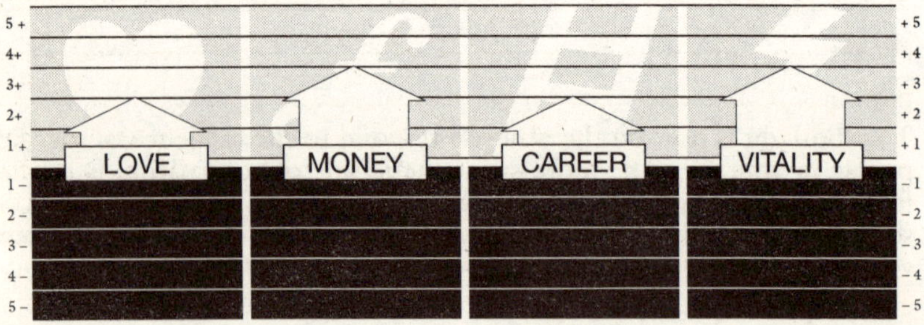

14 MONDAY *Moon Age Day 10 Moon Sign Aquarius*

am ....

pm ....

The emphasis now sits squarely on having fun and being able to express yourself fully. It's time to put the less favourable days of earlier in the month behind you, and to show other people how optimistic you can be. This in itself should go much of the way to helping you feel happy with your lot.

15 TUESDAY *Moon Age Day 11 Moon Sign Pisces*

am ....

pm ....

Get together with others as much as you can today. Scorpio can afford to be in a very sociable frame of mind, and should relish not only the proximity but also the opinions that the social maelstrom can offer. There may not be too much time to address work, but is that really your top priority at the moment?

16 WEDNESDAY *Moon Age Day 12 Moon Sign Pisces*

am ....

pm ....

If you feel that a sense of team spirit is lacking, that is part of what you need to put back into your life as soon as you can. It's a question of finding people with whom you could really co-operate, plus a few individuals who have it in their power to boost your success rate. This is definitely a day to keep your eyes open.

17 THURSDAY *Moon Age Day 13 Moon Sign Pisces*

am ....

pm ....

You can really make things happen right now. Instead of waiting for events to turn in your direction, take life by the hand and lead it where you wish. Make sure your charisma remains undiminished and that you are displaying the most attractive qualities of your zodiac sign. You need to capitalise on these positive trends.

18 FRIDAY *Moon Age Day 14 Moon Sign Aries*

am ....

pm ....

This has potential to be a favourable time for getting along with others in any situation. There is no need to be coy if you wish to put your point of view forward, even in unfamiliar situations. It's a mistake to assume that your opinions will be derided or rejected. On the contrary, it's an ideal opportunity to make new allies.

19 SATURDAY *Moon Age Day 15 Moon Sign Aries*

am ....

pm ....

Your social environment offers you scope to engineer encounters that you should find particularly interesting this weekend. You can make best use of these trends by arranging gatherings at home, or outings with friends this evening. Your powers of attraction are highlighted now.

20 SUNDAY *Moon Age Day 16 Moon Sign Taurus*

am ....

pm ....

The lunar low encourages you to keep life as simple as possible this Sunday. Even if the chilly winds are on their way, it wouldn't do any harm at all to get a little fresh air and a change of scene. Failing this, you need to find some quiet and yet rewarding way to pass on a few hours, possibly with family members.

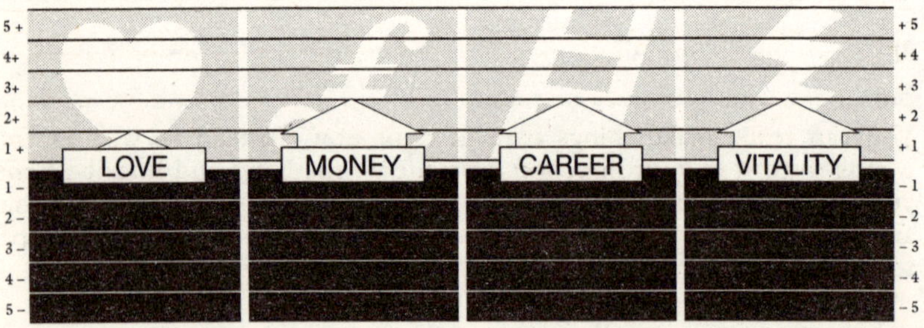

21 MONDAY ☿ *Moon Age Day 17 Moon Sign Taurus*

am ....

pm ....

Another slightly quieter day, though one that has potential to be funnier than you might expect. What you have at present is an ability to see the humour in almost any situation. Just make certain that if friends are involved, they don't think you are laughing directly at them. It's quite easy to upset others!

22 TUESDAY ☿ *Moon Age Day 18 Moon Sign Gemini*

am ....

pm ....

There is much to be said for choosing to spend some time thinking about personal matters that need special attention. With a slight pause in the general forward momentum of life and a contemplative mood possible, fairly lengthy periods of concentrated pondering are the order of the day for Scorpio now.

23 WEDNESDAY ☿ *Moon Age Day 19 Moon Sign Gemini*

am ....

pm ....

When it comes to most aspects of life at the moment, it's natural to want to have your cake and eat it too. Who wouldn't? However, it really isn't possible for most of the time. Be content with your lot, while at the same time hanging on to those aspirations for the future. Make sure you remember that life doesn't owe any of us a living.

24 THURSDAY ☿ *Moon Age Day 20 Moon Sign Gemini*

am ....

pm ....

There is plenty of scope for mutual assistance and a general sense of harmony now. Although the pensive side of your nature is still emphasised, your curiosity could also be raised significantly. This can encourage you to do some digging and delving, requiring more communication with the world at large.

25 FRIDAY ☿ *Moon Age Day 21 Moon Sign Cancer*

am...

pm...

Are issues from the past diverting your mind from the jobs at hand? If this is the case, your present tendency to analyse things too much could well be the cause. Gradually, as the day goes on, you should be in a position to move out of your own world, into the tangible one beyond your door.

26 SATURDAY ☿ *Moon Age Day 22 Moon Sign Cancer*

am...

pm...

Another boost to all matters associated with communication is available, and you should feel the wind of change blowing. It's time to tackle any jobs that have been waiting for a while, and you needn't let yourself be restricted by anyone who is trying to hold you back. Be prepared to show the charitable side of your nature.

27 SUNDAY ☿ *Moon Age Day 23 Moon Sign Leo*

am...

pm...

Even if there are few possibilities for having your ego massaged today, you simply have to get on and do things all the same. Deciding how you want to spend your free time could be your most difficult task under current influences. This is especially relevant if everyone around you is trying to attract your attention!

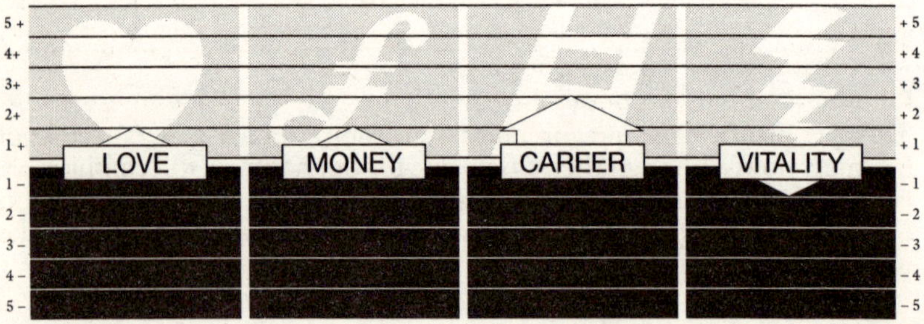

28 MONDAY ☿ *Moon Age Day 24 Moon Sign Leo*

am ....

pm ....

A new phase of dynamism and activity is available. Go for gold today, and make certain that absolutely everyone knows who you are and what you want from life. Scorpio should be entertaining, keen to talk to almost anyone and anxious to let the world know what it believes about a host of issues.

29 TUESDAY ☿ *Moon Age Day 25 Moon Sign Leo*

am ....

pm ....

Better progress is possible today, and especially so if you are a working Scorpio individual. Be prepared to support friends, particularly those who are having difficulties at present. Analysing their possible problems is one aspect of the process. Fortunately, your tolerance level should be quite high at the present time.

30 WEDNESDAY ☿ *Moon Age Day 26 Moon Sign Virgo*

am ....

pm ....

Emotional relationships are potentially good, but a few misunderstandings are a distinct possibility. It is very important to make sure that you are understood by your partner or others you care about deeply. There ought to be no real problem, particularly if you are using your powers of communication to the full now.

31 THURSDAY ☿ *Moon Age Day 27 Moon Sign Virgo*

am ....

pm ....

It's important to keep up with news regarding personal matters, though it's always possible that this will fail to materialise. If so, you will simply have to show some patience. Keeping confidences is vital if you want to convince others to trust you. They're unlikely to do this if you have been giving away secrets.

1 FRIDAY ☿ *Moon Age Day 28 Moon Sign Libra*

am ....

pm ....

Today is a chance for you to consider the benefits of group situations. This week hasn't been the ideal time for such activities, particularly if you have been concentrating on issues that mainly affect you. The forthcoming weekend offers you the chance to share – both material possessions and yourself.

2 SATURDAY ☿ *Moon Age Day 0 Moon Sign Libra*

am ....

pm ....

Are you tempted to empty your pocket on expensive things you don't require? That fine, though before every proposed purchase it's worth looking carefully and deciding whether this is something you actually do need. There are some startling new ideas on offer now, and you may well want to go for them all!

3 SUNDAY ☿ *Moon Age Day 1 Moon Sign Scorpio*

am ....

pm ....

Along come rewarding trends that are directly attributable to the lunar high. Confidence is highlighted, and this assists you to get on the road towards a more positive and fulfilling period, which really takes effect after the weekend. In the meantime, you can certainly afford to push your luck today.

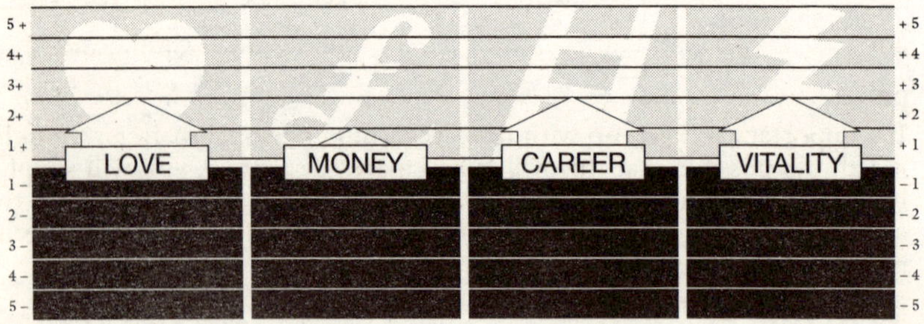

November 2013

Your Month at a Glance

(+) = Opportunities are around   (−) = Be on the defensive   (●) = Life is pretty ordinary

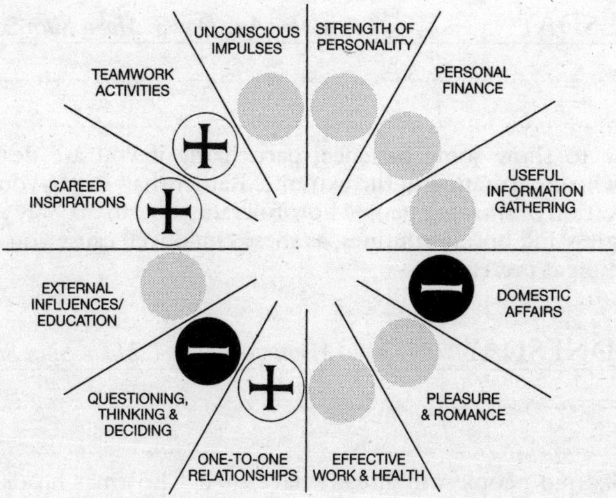

November Highs and Lows

Here I show you how the rhythms of the Moon will affect you this month. Like the tide, your energies and abilities will rise and fall with its pattern. When it is above the centre line, go for it, when it is below, you should be resting.

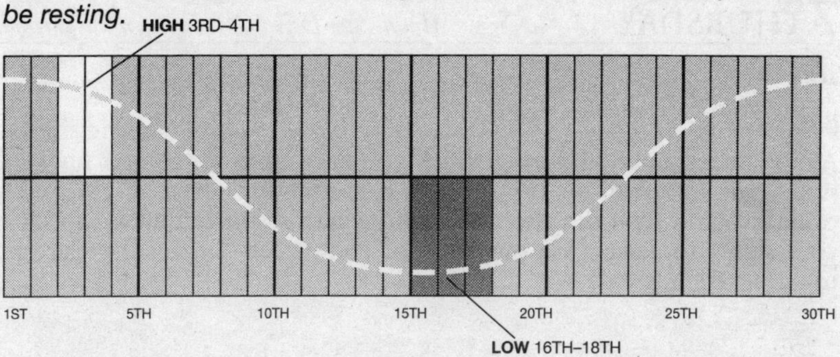

4 MONDAY ☿ *Moon Age Day 2 Moon Sign Scorpio*

am ....

pm ....

The lunar high continues to support your efforts to get ahead. You might feel that on a Monday these should all be geared towards professional matters but this needn't prevent you from having fun, or from making the most favourable impression imaginable on all types of people.

5 TUESDAY ☿ *Moon Age Day 3 Moon Sign Sagittarius*

am ....

pm ....

It's time to show some patience, particularly if you are dealing with people who are irritating in the extreme. Rather than losing your temper, it's a question of showing people how tolerant you can be. Stay away from meaningless and boring routines, as these could well cause you a sense of aggravation at present.

6 WEDNESDAY ☿ *Moon Age Day 4 Moon Sign Sagittarius*

am ....

pm ....

Many Scorpio people will already have their Christmas heads on, even though the event is still quite some time ahead. Normally, caution and patience would be advised, but not in the case of issues that simply have to be sorted out now. Keep working hard towards practical and professional objectives.

7 THURSDAY ☿ *Moon Age Day 5 Moon Sign Capricorn*

am ....

pm ....

Along comes a period during which you have a chance to pick up some significant information. It's time to pay attention, even to apparently casual remarks. You can also demonstrate your resourcefulness, as well as your ability to make a silk purse out of a sow's ear. These are great ways to attract friends!

8 FRIDAY ☿ *Moon Age Day 6 Moon Sign Capricorn*

am ....

pm ....

You seem to be in a commanding position with regard to the personality stakes. Make the most of these trends by socialising freely and by maintaining a high profile at work. However, you can't expect everyone to be as optimistic as you are. Support for others is the greatest gift you have to offer now.

9 SATURDAY ☿ *Moon Age Day 7 Moon Sign Aquarius*

am ....

pm ....

Take full advantage of a period during which forward planning is not only possible, but also enjoyable. Even if this isn't a crackerjack of a day, it does offer significantly better prospects money-wise. That doesn't necessarily mean you should be spending indiscriminately, although it's worth looking out for bargains.

10 SUNDAY ☿ *Moon Age Day 8 Moon Sign Aquarius*

am ....

pm ....

Trends suggest that some matters could come to a head now. If you were a salesperson the advice would be to close deals carefully. There is nothing wrong with your mental faculties, but you would be wise to think carefully before taking specific steps. Social mixing could allow you to gather views from a range of people.

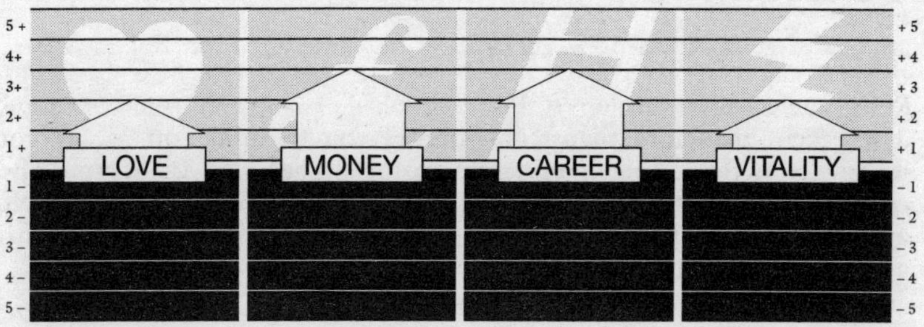

11 MONDAY ☿ *Moon Age Day 9 Moon Sign Aquarius*

am ....

pm ....

Significant input into areas of life you have stayed away from recently now seems to be on offer. Keeping busy is the name of the game, and you could well have little time to spare for frivolities. When it comes to the boring routines, see if you can persuade others to lend a hand – and make them more fun!

12 TUESDAY *Moon Age Day 10 Moon Sign Pisces*

am ....

pm ....

Once more minor opportunities to strengthen your finances are available. By all means keep an eye on what you are spending, but at the same time understand that you have to speculate a little in order to accumulate later on. Rewards of a social nature are within your grasp, particularly if you show how kind you can be.

13 WEDNESDAY *Moon Age Day 11 Moon Sign Pisces*

am ....

pm ....

The material side of life holds significant potential, even if it isn't easy to get everything you want. The midweek period is likely to be variable, and even somewhat odd at times. You can best further your long-term ambitions by seeking out and communicating with the right people at some stage today.

14 THURSDAY *Moon Age Day 12 Moon Sign Aries*

am ....

pm ....

The recent planetary thrust encourages you to fulfil your desire for luxury, something that is endemic to the zodiac sign of Scorpio. Be careful that you don't end up being accused of hedonism. A sociable approach still works best, and assists you to mix and mingle freely with all manner of people.

15 FRIDAY *Moon Age Day 13 Moon Sign Aries*

am ....

pm ....

Once again the spotlight is on efforts to strengthen your finances, and this might tempt you to spend a little more freely than would often be the case. Planning ahead works well now, especially with regard to any journeys you intend to make in the future. Patience is the key to success, and offers great gains – though not necessarily immediate ones.

16 SATURDAY *Moon Age Day 14 Moon Sign Taurus*

am ....

pm ....

Now that the lunar low has arrived, you may feel as though you are running out of steam. Since this is a Saturday, there might be more opportunities for you to take things easy and have a rest. If this proves to be impossible, there is much to be said for devoting a few hours to social matters and mixing freely with friends.

17 SUNDAY *Moon Age Day 15 Moon Sign Taurus*

am ....

pm ....

Keep to tried and tested paths for the moment, and bear in mind that so-called bargains might be nothing of the sort. If you have to make up your mind about anything, it pays to use your intuition, which remains generally strong around now. In many respects you are already well ahead of yourself, so be willing to dawdle.

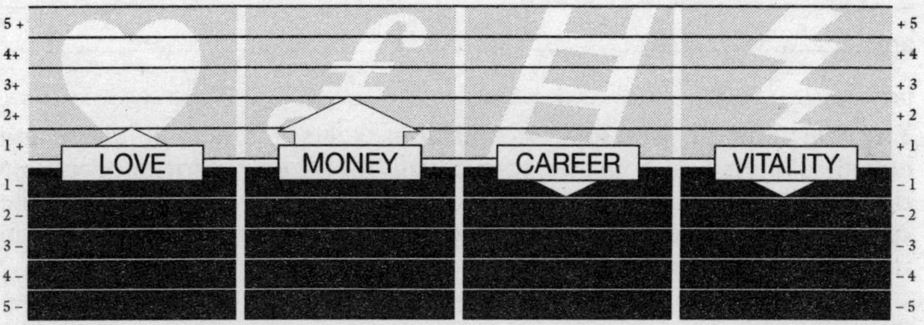

18 MONDAY *Moon Age Day 16 Moon Sign Taurus*

am ....

pm ....

You would be wise to stay away from boring routines as much as possible today, and should definitely gain from a change of scene. This applies just as much to the daylight hours as it does to social possibilities in the evening. Keeping confidences on behalf of others is essential, particularly if it is someone close to you.

19 TUESDAY *Moon Age Day 17 Moon Sign Gemini*

am ....

pm ....

By all means show your personality, but bear in mind that this can involve an excessive display of ego. The amount of planetary power that is available to you at present needs to be dealt with very carefully. The more you manage to stay on an even keel, the greater will be the number of potential gains you can attract.

20 WEDNESDAY *Moon Age Day 18 Moon Sign Gemini*

am ....

pm ....

You continue to possess a strong ability to direct your life in material matters, but might be less confident and successful when it comes to emotional concerns. The behaviour of others has a significant part to play in this situation, but you need to be clear about your own approach, regardless of what they are doing.

21 THURSDAY *Moon Age Day 19 Moon Sign Cancer*

am ....

pm ....

The Sun, now in your solar second house, acts as a new influence and one that offers you a chance to gradually build up securities. Certainly this could relate to money, but there are other possibilities too. The coming week also offers you an opportunity to consolidate your position in relationships.

22 FRIDAY *Moon Age Day 20 Moon Sign Cancer*

am ....

pm ....

Energy shouldn't be lacking, and neither is the ability to size up a situation and act immediately. It's time to bring into play your lightning-quick reactions and your strong ability to see clear through the minds of those around you. A day to show that Scorpio is more potent now than has been the case at any time this year.

23 SATURDAY *Moon Age Day 21 Moon Sign Leo*

am ....

pm ....

It seems that Scorpio can be the most dynamic and potentially lucky zodiac sign of the lot at present. Part of this is thanks to the position of the Sun in your solar chart, but it also relates to actions you took earlier in the year that are now beginning to mature. This should certainly add to your sense of success.

24 SUNDAY *Moon Age Day 22 Moon Sign Leo*

am ....

pm ....

If you want to find some relaxation today, trends encourage you to look towards home and family. Things should be more settled there than they are in your practical world, which is a potential maelstrom of activity. Give yourself time to reflect on recent happenings and avoid rushing anything for today if at all possible.

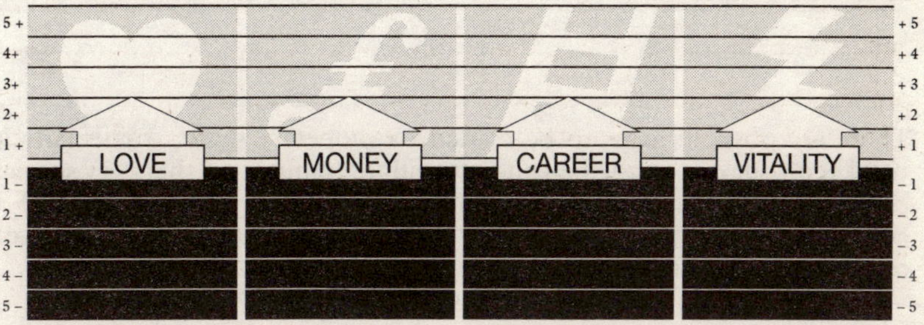

25 MONDAY *Moon Age Day 23 Moon Sign Leo*

am ....

pm ....

Getting practical matters into good working order should be a piece of cake today, and will leave you more time to please yourself. There really is no need to run around from pillar to post and you can genuinely afford to take a few hours out to be with those you love and to simply have a good time.

26 TUESDAY *Moon Age Day 24 Moon Sign Virgo*

am ....

pm ....

This would be an excellent day for staying in the thick of things generally and for blowing away any cobwebs that have accumulated. The way you behave now can help you to attract some positive attention, and might even allow you to make an impression on those who hold a particular fascination for you.

27 WEDNESDAY *Moon Age Day 25 Moon Sign Virgo*

am ....

pm ....

It pays to seek out the new and unusual in life if it proves possible to do so at the moment. Anything odd or even downright weird holds a real fascination for Scorpio, and especially so at the moment. In hard financial terms, there are rewards to be achieved through speculation with regard to specific objects.

28 THURSDAY *Moon Age Day 26 Moon Sign Libra*

am ....

pm ....

There are possible gains to be made in a monetary sense, particularly if you keep your eye on the ball and are willing to hunt out that very special bargain. Too much speculation isn't to be advised, but you can tell a confidence trick when you see one. Your ability to assess the sincerity of others is also enhanced now.

29 FRIDAY *Moon Age Day 27 Moon Sign Libra*

am ....

pm..

Friendship should be well highlighted for this Friday, which includes the attachments you feel for some family members too. There are benefits associated with food and drink, as well as the chance to pursue social activities that look particularly interesting, though you need to be willing to look in surprising directions.

30 SATURDAY *Moon Age Day 28 Moon Sign Libra*

am ....

pm..

There is much to be said for slackening the pace of life, though this might not please you too much if there is plenty going on around you. If you are at work, organisation is now the key. It should enable you to get the dross out of the way early and then enjoy the positive social and personal trends that are on offer.

1 SUNDAY *Moon Age Day 29 Moon Sign Scorpio*

am ....

pm..

Decision making should turn out to be far easier than previously now. The lunar high gives you every encouragement to mix with people you know can be good for you. Better luck is there for the taking, and you can afford to indulge yourself in the odd speculation, as long as the risk is a calculated one.

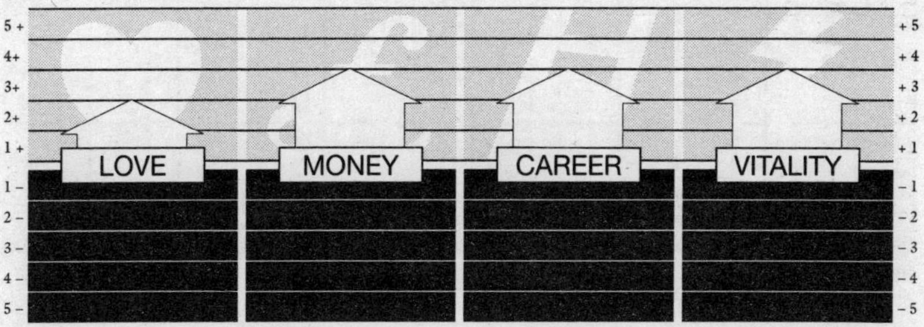

♏

December 2013

Your Month at a Glance

(+) = Opportunities are around (−) = Be on the defensive (●) = Life is pretty ordinary

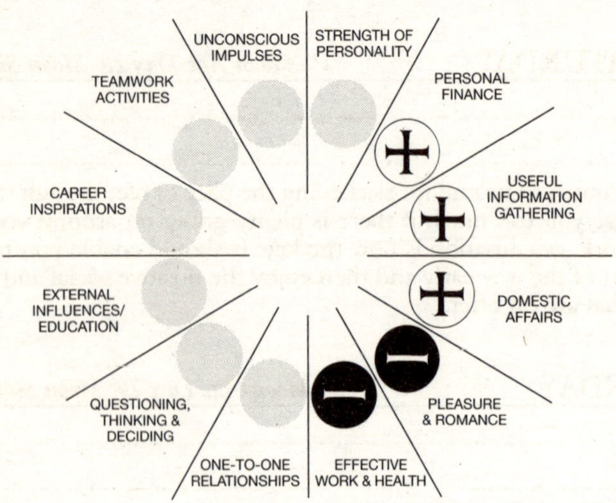

December Highs and Lows

Here I show you how the rhythms of the Moon will affect you this month. Like the tide, your energies and abilities will rise and fall with its pattern. When it is above the centre line, go for it, when it is below, you should be resting.

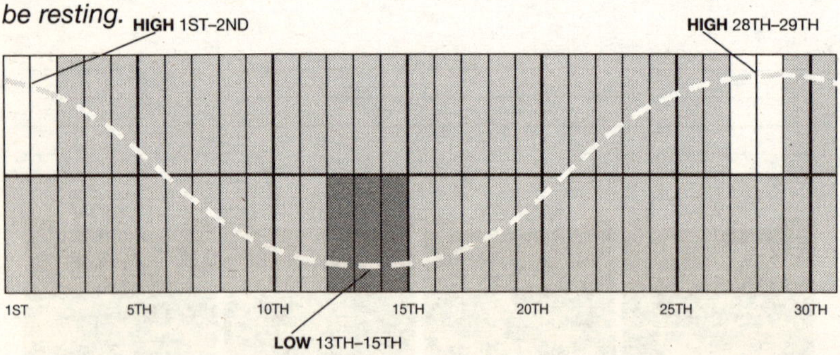

2 MONDAY *Moon Age Day 0 Moon Sign Scorpio*

am ....

pm ....

This has potential to be a very favourable moment for putting new plans into action. The message is that you shouldn't delay! The time is right to deal with money matters and to simplify specific areas of your life. Unnecessary spats at home are best avoided, no matter who is actually starting them.

3 TUESDAY *Moon Age Day 1 Moon Sign Sagittarius*

am ....

pm ....

Trends suggest that patience may not be your strong point at the moment. This is especially relevant in emotional attachments, where you could be dealing with frustrations of one sort or another. Maintaining a sense of proportion may not be easy, but is your chief necessity for today, and possibly even tomorrow.

4 WEDNESDAY *Moon Age Day 2 Moon Sign Sagittarius*

am ....

pm ....

Be prepared for the possibility of minor disappointments in your love life at this stage of the working week. Rather than allowing these to dominate your thinking, you need a cool head and strong reasoning ability. Sometimes it's necessary to allow time and your own changing attitude to put matters right.

5 THURSDAY *Moon Age Day 3 Moon Sign Capricorn*

am ....

pm ....

This may not be the easiest time to achieve a sense of fulfilment in emotional matters. Love is always present in your life, it's the human aspect of the situation that can be complicated. Maybe you are taking the things others are saying too literally, or even putting a slant on them that isn't really there.

6 FRIDAY *Moon Age Day 4 Moon Sign Capricorn*

am ....

pm..

This is an ideal time for capitalising on new opportunities, no matter in which direction you find them. You can't expect every line of enquiry that you follow at the moment to lead to great realisations. On the contrary, you may well have to dig deep into life at present to get to the truth of matters.

7 SATURDAY *Moon Age Day 5 Moon Sign Aquarius*

am ....

pm..

There are signs that the practical in life isn't quite so easy to address now as it was yesterday. This is particularly the case if you are tied to routines that you really can't get away from. Treat these with a little respect, but also find moments to have some fun. Financial gains might be available as the day wears on.

8 SUNDAY *Moon Age Day 6 Moon Sign Aquarius*

am ....

pm..

Slowly but surely you should have opportunities available to heat things up. Be prepared to dispel any frustration from early in the day and push through to some of your objectives. Make the most of this family period and do what you can to support the ideas and wishes of people who deserve your time and attention.

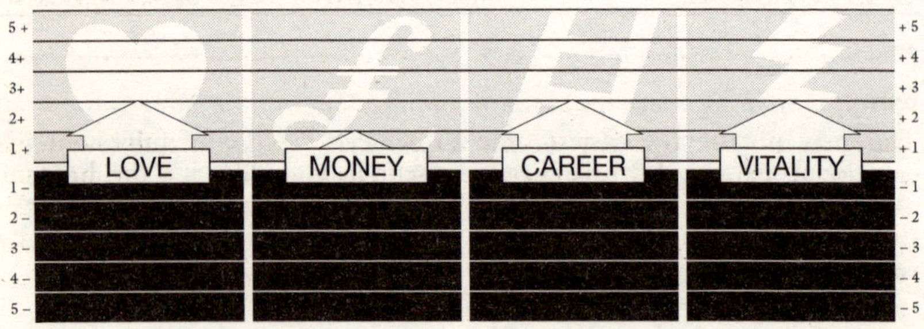

9 MONDAY *Moon Age Day 7 Moon Sign Pisces*

am ....

pm ....

When it comes to work and finance, you are in a position to capitalise on a quite beneficial sort of day. Even if it's difficult to bring any real excitement into your life at the moment, there is much to be said for planning, and for doing things that contribute to the festive period that lies immediately ahead of you.

10 TUESDAY *Moon Age Day 8 Moon Sign Pisces*

am ....

pm ....

Co-operative ventures are well accented early in the week, and could encourage you to put your ego to one side. The spotlight is now on your abilities as a very committed team player, and on your willingness to go with the flow. There are personal gains to be made ahead of Christmas, and new relationships on offer.

11 WEDNESDAY *Moon Age Day 9 Moon Sign Aries*

am ....

pm ....

You have scope to use your charm to persuade others to do whatever you wish. The fact is that those you really know well would deny you nothing. Of course you wouldn't dream of taking advantage of this situation, would you? In any case, today is about giving as much as you get in every direction today.

12 THURSDAY *Moon Age Day 10 Moon Sign Aries*

am ....

pm ....

In terms of everyday life, success today is about adapting to the needs and wants of others. The general level of excitement can be maintained, and there is little to prevent you from having a good time. Even if this period isn't exactly inspirational, it can offer you plenty of opportunities for information gathering.

13 FRIDAY *Moon Age Day 11 Moon Sign Taurus*

am ....

pm ....

It's time to recharge your batteries, which is quite sensible ahead of Christmas. Of course, you might think there is little time to slow things down, particularly if you have plenty of preparations to make. In the end you might be surprised at just how well you can persuade others to make some of the running.

14 SATURDAY *Moon Age Day 12 Moon Sign Taurus*

am ....

pm ....

Attempts to get on in life could lead to some disappointments, because the influence of that rather negative Moon is still present. Keep your expectations reasonably low and settle for a quiet time. The start of the weekend might not prove to be especially exciting, but it can lead to some unexpected gains.

15 SUNDAY *Moon Age Day 13 Moon Sign Taurus*

am ....

pm ....

This is not the most favourable day for exercising sound judgement. It's important for you to recognise the risk of being misled, something you would want to avoid at all cost. In family relationships, a careful and honest approach works best in discussions. Be ready to respond to the needs of friends at this time.

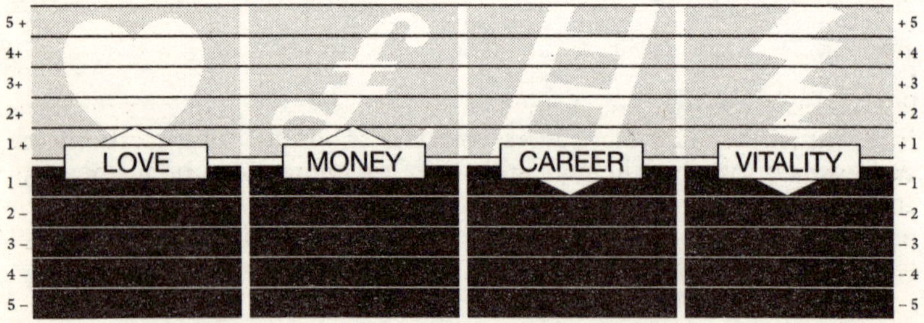

16 MONDAY *Moon Age Day 14 Moon Sign Gemini*

am ....

pm ....

There is an increasing focus on your ego, particularly if something you have done recently gives you cause to be proud of yourself. Don't let this fact go to your head because pride definitely does go before a fall. You should be in a position to offer timely help and help to those around you who need it now.

17 TUESDAY *Moon Age Day 15 Moon Sign Gemini*

am ....

pm ....

A day for getting things together and being willing to show how creative you can be at the moment. Perhaps you are taking an hour or two out to create decorations for the Christmas tree or balancing on a ladder to put up the fairy lights. One thing is for certain – you don't need to take life too seriously today.

18 WEDNESDAY *Moon Age Day 16 Moon Sign Cancer*

am ....

pm ....

Your fun-loving side is still well accented. This is an excellent day for personal relationships and for pursuing your objectives in a material sense. Shopping sprees would be an ideal activity, and there is much to be said for leaving a few specific jobs on the back burner just for the moment.

19 THURSDAY *Moon Age Day 17 Moon Sign Cancer*

am ....

pm ....

Ask yourself whether you are trying to do too many things at the same time. Is this becoming a habit that you need to address? Make sure you are displaying the most attractive aspects of your personality at the moment. In particular, you should be able to impress others with all the genuine magnetism you generate.

20 FRIDAY *Moon Age Day 18 Moon Sign Cancer*

am ....

pm ....

Seek out change and diversity for its own sake today. The end of the year is not far off, and this is a time that can sometimes be typified by negativity, which is a shame. The more you vary your routines and the greater the number of things you are aiming for, the more positive experience you should have today.

21 SATURDAY *Moon Age Day 19 Moon Sign Leo*

am ....

pm ....

There are entertaining experiences available this weekend. Trends encourage you to put yourself in the limelight at the moment, so you may decide that it's your personal task to create much of the fun in your vicinity. If you are well ahead with your work, you can certainly take some time out to do what pleases you.

22 SUNDAY *Moon Age Day 20 Moon Sign Leo*

am ....

pm ....

Bright ideas are the name of the game at present. What may be lacking is the necessary energy to put many of them into practice. Although you will want to make the running socially, even here you could run out of steam. By tomorrow you can get yourself back to normal, and in the meantime, simply watch life go by.

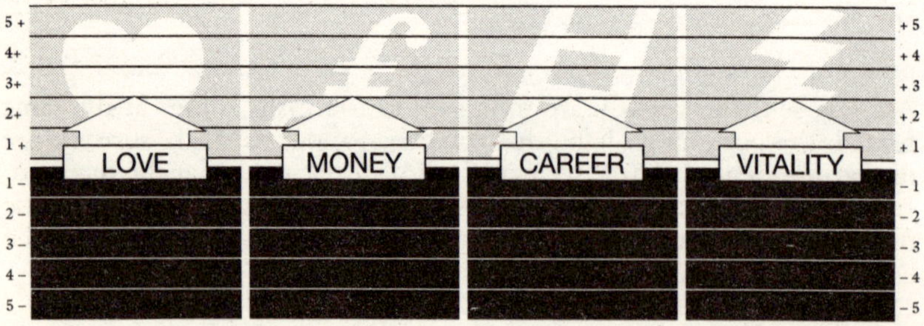

23 MONDAY *Moon Age Day 21 Moon Sign Virgo*

am ....

pm ....

All sorts of communications are emphasised today, and it's up to you to make the very best of this interlude. This might involve using every possible means to keep in touch, even with loved ones who are far away. Conforming to physical expectations could be somewhat tricky under current planetary influences.

24 TUESDAY *Moon Age Day 22 Moon Sign Virgo*

am ....

pm ....

With the accent on action and the big day just around the corner, you may feel you are trying to fit a quart into a pint pot today. If you've made sure you are well prepared, you should be able to ensure that the festive season goes with a swing for everyone concerned. Romantic potential is particularly emphasised now.

25 WEDNESDAY *Moon Age Day 23 Moon Sign Virgo*

am ....

pm ....

Christmas Day calls for a positive approach, and you need to be prepared to tackle the domestic demands of the day. It pays to be on your best behaviour and to show the naturally affectionate side of your zodiac sign. By all means find fun in situations, though take care that your sense of humour doesn't cause offence.

26 THURSDAY *Moon Age Day 24 Moon Sign Libra*

am ....

pm ....

As Boxing Day dawns, you can afford to opt for a slightly quieter day, though one that offers a chance for you to get in touch with people you might not normally see over Christmas, including colleagues. Those Scorpions who have the option of travel today might turn out to be the luckiest of all.

27 FRIDAY *Moon Age Day 25 Moon Sign Libra*

am ....

pm..

Be prepared to deal with some ups and downs at home, though that doesn't mean you can't maintain your sense of humour. You might even manage to make some mischief yourself! Keep a look-out for positive information relating to family issues, some of which could be quite surprising. Scorpio can be very creative now.

28 SATURDAY *Moon Age Day 26 Moon Sign Scorpio*

am ....

pm..

Positive thinking pays handsome dividends and should leave nobody in any doubt as to your state of mind. The lunar high supports your schemes, and assists you to persuade the people with whom you associate to lend a hand. Even romantic issues can be lightened and brightened significantly now.

29 SUNDAY *Moon Age Day 27 Moon Sign Scorpio*

am ....

pm..

Your luck is in, and you really need to exploit it to the full. Part of this relates to the positive impression you can make on others, which could in turn could convince them to put their trust in you. If Christmas celebrations are still on the go for Scorpio, you might be tempted to burn the midnight oil!

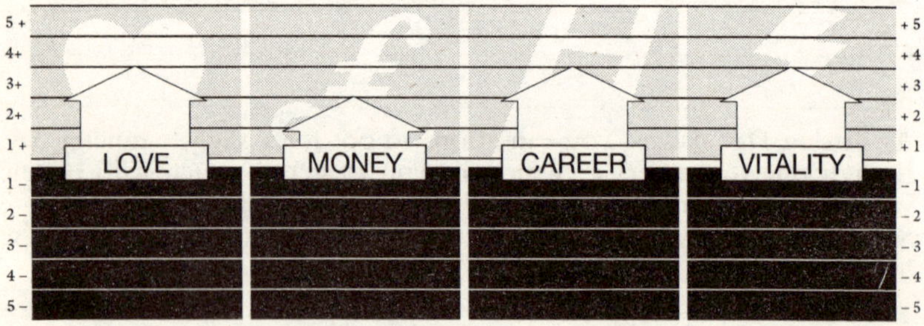

30 MONDAY *Moon Age Day 28 Moon Sign Sagittarius*

am..

pm..

A hectic pace is not only a possibility today – it's a necessity! What matters most is communication. You have what it takes to talk the hind leg off a donkey, but if you can't find one of those, almost anyone will do! Even people you barely pass the time of day with as a rule could now be targets for your tongue.

31 TUESDAY *Moon Age Day 29 Moon Sign Sagittarius*

am..

pm..

The last day of the year calls for a community-minded approach, and you should be willing to lend a hand whenever you can. Charity is writ large within you today, and that might even extend to raising money for a specific cause that is close to your heart. By the evening, you can afford to devote your time to having fun.

RISING SIGNS FOR SCORPIO

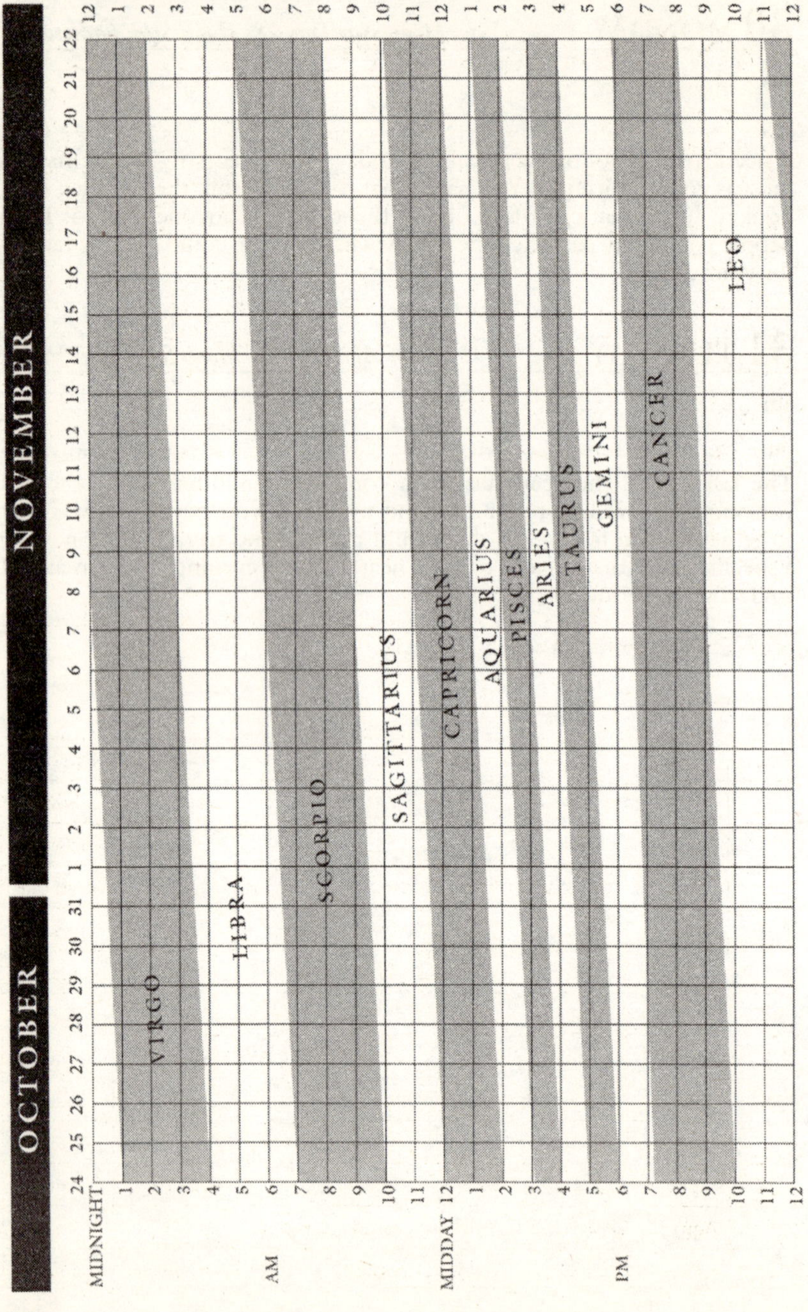

THE ZODIAC, PLANETS AND CORRESPONDENCES

The Earth revolves around the Sun once every calendar year, so when viewed from Earth the Sun appears in a different part of the sky as the year progresses. In astrology, these parts of the sky are divided into the signs of the zodiac and this means that the signs are organised in a circle. The circle begins with Aries and ends with Pisces.

Taking the zodiac sign as a starting point, astrologers then work with all the positions of planets, stars and many other factors to calculate horoscopes and birth charts and tell us what the stars have in store for us.

The table below shows the planets and Elements for each of the signs of the zodiac. Each sign belongs to one of the four Elements: Fire, Air, Earth or Water. Fire signs are creative and enthusiastic; Air signs are mentally active and thoughtful; Earth signs are constructive and practical; Water signs are emotional and have strong feelings.

It also shows the metals and gemstones associated with, or corresponding with, each sign. The correspondence is made when a metal or stone possesses properties that are held in common with a particular sign of the zodiac.

Finally, the table shows the opposite of each star sign – this is the opposite sign in the astrological circle.

Placed	Sign	Symbol	Element	Planet	Metal	Stone	Opposite
1	Aries	Ram	Fire	Mars	Iron	Bloodstone	Libra
2	Taurus	Bull	Earth	Venus	Copper	Sapphire	Scorpio
3	Gemini	Twins	Air	Mercury	Mercury	Tiger's Eye	Sagittarius
4	Cancer	Crab	Water	Moon	Silver	Pearl	Capricorn
5	Leo	Lion	Fire	Sun	Gold	Ruby	Aquarius
6	Virgo	Maiden	Earth	Mercury	Mercury	Sardonyx	Pisces
7	Libra	Scales	Air	Venus	Copper	Sapphire	Aries
8	Scorpio	Scorpion	Water	Pluto	Plutonium	Jasper	Taurus
9	Sagittarius	Archer	Fire	Jupiter	Tin	Topaz	Gemini
10	Capricorn	Goat	Earth	Saturn	Lead	Black Onyx	Cancer
11	Aquarius	Waterbearer	Air	Uranus	Uranium	Amethyst	Leo
12	Pisces	Fishes	Water	Neptune	Tin	Moonstone	Virgo